What We Believe

The Beauty of the Catholic Faith

Marcellino D'Ambrosio and Andrew Swafford

ASCENSION

West Chester, Pennsylvania

Nihil obstat: Rev. Msgr. Joseph G. Prior, STD
                  Censor librorum
                  May 11, 2022

Imprimatur: + Most Reverend Nelson J. Pérez
                  Archbishop of Philadelphia
                  April 20, 2022

Ascension
PO Box 1990
West Chester, PA 19380
1-800-376-0520
ascensionpress.com

Cover Design: Stella Ziegler
Cover Art: Monica Skrzypczak, Outpouring of Trust
Interior Design: Sarah Stueve

Printed in United States of America

ISBN: 978-1-954881-45-7

CONTENTS

Introduction. 1

Part I: Who We Are 3
Chapter 1: The Family of God 5

Chapter 2: Our Catholic Heritage. 17

Chapter 3: Faith and Reason. 27

Chapter 4: A Journey and a Commitment 37

Part II: Our Faith 45
Chapter 5: One God, the Father Almighty. 47

Chapter 6: Creation and the Fall. 57

Chapter 7: Jesus, God with Us 69

Chapter 8: Jesus Christ, Redeemer .81

Chapter 9: The Breath of God 91

Chapter 10: The Spirit and the Bride 101

Part III: Our Life. 113
Chapter 11: Liturgy and Sacraments. 115

Chapter 12: The Eucharist: Sacrament of Sacraments 127

Chapter 13: Catholic Spirituality and the Call to Holiness 141

Chapter 14: Prayer, Liturgy, and Devotion 155

Chapter 15: Fasting: Making Room for God 167

Chapter 16: Almsgiving: A Lifestyle of Mercy. 179

Conclusion: Life Everlasting 193

Introduction

Many today view Christianity as a belief system. But Christianity is better understood as a story—the story of a relationship.

All the major Christian churches agree on the basics of the story as recorded in the Bible. Though created for intimate friendship with God, the human race, from the beginning, chose to go its own way, cutting itself off from its Creator. The misery and death that resulted from this broken relationship could only be overcome by God's initiative.

And so God sent his eternal Son as a man, Jesus of Nazareth. By his act of total self-giving on the Cross, Jesus atoned for our sins and reconciled us to God, his Father. By rising from the dead, he liberated us from death's power and offered us a share in God's own inner life—a glorious life that lasts forever. The Good News announced ever since is that this intimate life with God through his Holy Spirit is available to anyone who will accept it.

This is the *kerygma*, the basic gospel proclamation at the center of Christianity.

But what about "Catholicism?" What do saints, sacraments, and hierarchy have to do with a personal relationship with God in Christ? After all, many Christians seem to get along just fine without these Catholic distinctions.

This book does not attempt to give an exhaustive account of Catholic faith and life. But it does aim to get to the very heart of what the term "catholic" actually means. So this book will outline *who we are* as Catholics, *what we believe*, and *how we live*. In the process, it will become apparent that things considered by some to be Catholic "extras" are instead integral to the fullness of truth and life that Jesus came to bring us.

Jesus is "the way, and the truth, and the life" (John 14:6), and the early Christians were known for being people of the "Way."[1] This is important for us to keep in mind as we seek, in the course of this book, to retrieve the sense of Catholic Christianity as a way of life. For the Catholic Faith is not a mere "philosophy" or set of ideas, let alone merely another political interest group. Rather, being Catholic means making a journey into the heart of God not as isolated individuals, but in the company of a family that Jesus called the Church (see Matthew 16:18). This New Covenant family of faith is a mysterious fellowship intended by God to satisfy the deep longing of our hearts not only for union with God but for that deep communion with other people that we often call community.

This is who we are as Catholic Christians. This identity animates a way of believing and a way of living—the Catholic way. Our lives are not our own; we have been "bought with a price" (1 Corinthians 6:20). And the "gift" of our lives—like that of our Lord Jesus Christ—is meant to be joyfully lived with and for others.

Jesus wants our joy to be full (see John 15:11). He came that we might have life and have it abundantly (see John 10:10). The word *catholic* actually comes from a Greek word meaning "whole" or "full." The Catholic way is all about the whole truth leading to the fullest, deepest, most life-giving relationship possible—with both God our Father and with our brothers and sisters in Christ. In what follows, we invite you to join us as we explore our common inheritance, "the unsearchable riches of Christ" (Ephesians 3:8), which he has entrusted in the Spirit to his Church.

A Note about This Book and the What We Believe Study Program

This book has three parts: (I) Who We Are, (II) Our Faith, and (III) Our Life. As Catholics, we subscribe to more than a set of beliefs. We are part of a Church, a communion of Christ's faithful, and we strive to live our lives according to the teachings of Christ and his Church. Our identity, our beliefs, and our practices are what make us Catholic.

While this book is written so that you can read it on its own, it is also part of a larger study program, which includes a ten-part video series, a workbook, and a chart. This book and the larger program provide an excellent overview of Catholic beliefs and practices. The material is ideal both for Catholics who wish to better understand and explain their Faith and for those who are interested in entering the Catholic Church.

PART I

Who We Are

For by one Spirit we were all baptized into one body. ... If one member suffers, all suffer together; if one member is honored, all rejoice together.

—1 Corinthians 12:13, 26

CHAPTER 1

The Family of God

Loneliness has always been a problem in human history. But in today's post-Christian world, loneliness and isolation have grown to epidemic proportions. And we see that, despite all efforts to the contrary, strife between nations, races, and political parties continues to assume one new virulent form after another.

The biblical story actually explains the root of all this. God's plan was for humanity to be one big, happy family. Adam was to be the patriarch, and Eve the mother of all the living. But these two chose to disobey God. Ironically, the very first effect of this collaboration was division between them. Sin actually spoiled their own perfect intimacy, introducing into their relationship all the misunderstandings and problems between the sexes with which we are all too familiar (see Genesis 3).

They had been tricked. Satan, the Father of Lies, is also the master of alienation. Sin is all about division—from God, from one another, and even within the heart of each person. The divisive, isolating impact of sin is seen most dramatically in the story of the Tower of Babel. This time, it is all of Adam and Eve's descendants who join together in exalting themselves in opposition to God. This decision, instead of bringing them closer together, drives them apart, scattering them into peoples who can no longer either understand or tolerate each other.

So a savior was needed not just to reconcile each sinner individually to their Creator but to "gather into one the children of God who are scattered"

(John 11:52). Pentecost, the birthday of this new, reconciled people, was a reverse of Babel; the crowd that gathered to see what all the commotion was about were from "every nation under heaven" (Acts 2:5). Yet they each heard the same, unifying message proclaimed in their own language. And so thousands of people from far-flung corners of the globe were unified by being joined to the excited group of Jesus' followers.

As the Good News spread from Jerusalem to other cities, the disciples of Jesus were called Christians for the first time in Antioch (see Acts 11:26). A few decades later, the term "catholic" first appeared in the writings of Ignatius, the second bishop of Antioch. But, for him and subsequent Fathers of the Church, the term catholic was never a noun referring to a follower of Jesus of Nazareth. It was an adjective used to describe a quality of the Church that Jesus founded—the Catholic Church. So, before we examine the definition of the term catholic, the first question to ask is: How do you define "the Church"?

The answer is that you really can't because the Church is more than a human reality. Given that it is a creation of the Holy Spirit, it is a supernatural mystery so full of meaning that it exceeds our powers of understanding. This mystery that is the Church can only be approached through symbols and images. All of these images are analogies drawn from Scripture and illumined by human experience. As beautiful and provocative as they may be, they are each, by themselves, inadequate. To compensate for this, God provides us with many of them—ninety-six can be found in the New Testament![2]

These manifold images complement one another and together help disclose the richness of the Church's nature, revealing it as an answer to one of our deepest needs: the need for community. In this chapter, we will explore just three of the most important master images and notice how they help us make sense of the Catholic Church.

Family of God

The New Testament's most common image for the Church is probably the family. Everywhere in the epistles, Christians are addressed as brothers and sisters. Other verses identify the Church as the household of God (see Ephesians 2:19 and 1 Peter 4:17). And, every time we repeat the prayer that Jesus taught us, saying "Our Father," we are reminded that we are a family. Jesus shares his Father with us, making himself the "first-born" of many "brothers and sisters." He also gives us his Holy Spirit—the family bond that binds us together. And, since no family is complete without a mother, one of Jesus' final acts in this world was to bequeath to us his own mother (see John 19:26–27).

To be Catholic is to enter this family, to be *received* into a family—the family of God stretching back through the apostles and prophets to Abraham and Sarah. To be Catholic is to realize that this great story did not end with the death of the last apostle or with the completion of the last book in what we now call the New Testament. Rather, the story continues, and we stand waist-deep in the stream of salvation history. The New Covenant (or "New Testament"), then, is primarily a *living* familial reality, not just an ancient set of documents.

Implications of Family

In any family, relationships are primary. People marry to have intimacy with each other and with the children God sends them. Yet, given that we are human beings with bodily needs, our relationships need to be supported by a certain amount of what we call institution. Marriage, in fact, is an institution. A married couple has a legal status, pays taxes, owns or rents a dwelling, and bequeaths their estate to children and grandchildren. However, all these institutional aspects of marital life are ultimately at the service of relationships.

That is the way it is with this spiritual family, the Church. Though the whole point of the Church is a living communion with God and one another, it needs a certain amount of institutional reality to sustain family life this side of heaven.

Sadly, it is undeniable that there have been times in Catholic life when institution has been put ahead of relationship. This is unfortunate, but it is the kind of thing that can happen in any family. The problem is not solved by abolishing the institution. It would not make sense to suggest that a couple having marriage trouble solve their problems by getting rid of their house, their cars, and all their assets. Rather, a wise counselor would encourage them to dwell less on their "stuff" and put more time and effort into renewing their relationship. The same is true within the Church. Instead of firing away at the Church as an institution, we need to play our part in renewing the Church as a family.

Authority is another related dimension of family life that characterizes the Church. A family has elders—parents, grandparents, uncles, and aunts. You come to realize that they have their weak spots and their quirks. But they also have important wisdom to share and an indispensable role to play.

The Church, too, has elders—ordained leaders who help God's family mature and grow. In fact, the word "priest" comes from the Greek term *presbyter*, which means "elder." The priest is an elder member of the family who bears authority not only because of his training and experience but also because he has been commissioned and anointed to serve and lead the family.

The familial character of the Church is also shown by the fact that we call our priests "father," a practice that reflects the thinking within the early Church. St. Paul spoke of his fatherly care for the Corinthians: "For though you have countless guides in Christ, you do not have many fathers. For I became your father in Christ Jesus through the gospel" (1 Corinthians 4:15).

For Catholics today, the person in whom this role of fatherly care and authority is most universally invested is the pope. Interestingly, that is what the very word "pope" means: it is an English word coming from *papa*, meaning "father." In Spanish and Italian, this is the precise title for the successor of St. Peter. The pope is the father of the universal Catholic family, just as the bishop is the father of the diocese, and the pastor and his assistant priests are the fathers of the local parish communities.

So what about the church building? It is very much the family dwelling. This is brought out clearly by the Italian word for cathedral—*duomo*—which comes from the Latin *domus,* meaning "home." As important as such buildings are, however, we must remember that the smallest pastoral unit of the Church is not the parish but the family—the "domestic church." Parents, as Sts. Thomas Aquinas and Pope John Paul II tell us, have a pastoral office not unlike that of parish priests.[3] While the sacraments are not typically celebrated in the home, the Christian family is the first and primary place where, in God's design, children learn to pray, serve, and love.

Likewise, the many ceremonies of the Catholic Church can be understood as family celebrations. The Eucharist is a holy sacrifice, but it is also our family meal, celebrating and deepening our bond with the Lord and one another. Baptism, Confirmation, Matrimony, Holy Orders, and the Anointing of the Sick—all of these consecrate special moments in our family life.

A Holy Nation

The Church can also be described as a people, "a holy nation, God's own people" (1 Peter 2:9). God intervened in the family of Abraham, Isaac, and Jacob and gradually built them up into a nation. It was an imperfect nation, to be sure—just look at the kings of Israel for a study of failed leadership! Still, it was God's nation, God's people.

We are a family that has grown into a nation whose king, ruler, and lord is Jesus the Messiah. But we are a universal nation, not a particular ethnic group. This, in fact, is one of the meanings of the term catholic, as we will see in our next chapter. What are the elements that constitute this nation, the people of God? Let us explore just a few of them.

Nations Have Heroes

Especially through its schools, a nation makes it a priority to teach its citizens about their history and about the heroes who embody the nation's essence and ideals. In the Catholic Church, the liturgy pays particular attention to the saints—those great heroes and heroines who show us what God's nation is really about and what we are destined to become. Certainly, all of us who are Christians are, in a certain sense, saints; all of us are sons and daughters of God. But this is often hard to detect when we look at ourselves and most other Christians we know.

This hit me (Marcellino D'Ambrosio) in a poignant way during a visit to the Accademia Gallery in Florence, Italy, where I saw some rather strange statues by Michelangelo on my way down the corridor to see his spectacular sculpture of David. They were unfinished statues of figures who looked like they were entrapped in blocks of stone, struggling to emerge. I found them mildly interesting only because I knew who the sculptor was, and I breezed by them rather quickly. But then I got to the end of the hall to where Michelangelo's statue of David is displayed. I suddenly understood where the artist was going with those hunks of marble I had just passed by so nonchalantly! After admiring the statue of David, I rushed back to them and, finally, could appreciate their noble beauty as works in progress.

That is the way it is with us and the saints. We are works in progress; the saints are the finished masterpieces who point to what we are called to become. In studying and celebrating their lives, we come to understand our own call and dignity.

Two thousand years' worth of saints are already in heavenly glory, so we who are still struggling in this world are just the tip of the iceberg, the visible but smaller part of God's "holy nation." Part of what it means to be Catholic, then, is to get to know these many heroes of the Faith who have been made holy, perfect, and spotless. We can read their lives and their writings to help us stay on course in running the same race they did. We can keep their statues and pictures around as nations do with their heroes. For us, though, such representations are not just an encouragement to imitation; they are a reminder that the saints are gloriously alive in Christ and that they pray constantly for us.

National Holidays

Nations observe holidays. These celebrations of people and events bind citizens together, reinforce identity, and strengthen unity. Similarly, in the Catholic Church, we have holy days that unite us more closely with each other and with Jesus, our captain and the greatest hero of all. Moving through these yearly celebrations from Advent to Pentecost, we enter more and more deeply into Jesus' birth, death, and glorious resurrection. The

Church year also includes a regular cycle of celebrations of its heroes and heroines, many of whom "made the supreme sacrifice."

Nations Need Government

Every nation needs government. Christ knew this, and so he personally chose twelve apostles[4] on whom to establish the Church. Why twelve? Because Israel as a nation was founded on twelve foundation stones—the twelve patriarchs. Jesus was founding a renewed and reconstituted Israel, so he chose twelve men from among his disciples, and he gave them a special responsibility that no one else had.

This unique role stands out in Scripture in both the Gospels and the Acts of the Apostles, both in Jesus' lifetime and afterward. The apostles were the ones called to serve as the official witnesses of Jesus' resurrection (see Acts 1:22). They were the spokesmen. Together, they were the united body that led the Church, and they made important decisions about its direction (see Acts 15:6). The apostles themselves ordained men (see Acts 14:23) whom they called bishops (Greek for "overseers") or presbyters (Greek for "elders"). Those men, in turn, handed on their ministry to others, training them and entrusting to them the ministry of teaching and guiding (see 2 Timothy 2:2). Clearly, it was Christ's intent to provide for an orderly succession of pastors to lead the Church. That is what apostolic succession is all about: it is the unbroken chain from Christ to the apostles and to their successors through the centuries, down to the present-day bishops of the Catholic Church.

It is important to note that the Church does not put these men *over* the Bible. As the Second Vatican Council noted, these leaders are *under* the authority of God's Word and are subject to it, like every other follower of Christ.[5] Their job is to serve the Word of God by teaching and interpreting it so that we can take it as the guide of our lives without falling into all sorts of distortions and wrong turns.

For me (D'Ambrosio), this principle was beautifully illustrated at the funeral of Pope St. Paul VI, one of the twentieth century's greatest popes, who had the hard and often thankless task of completing and implementing the

Second Vatican Council. On the day of the funeral, a magnificent assembly of dignitaries from all over the world gathered in St. Peter's Square, along with cardinals and bishops in full regalia. It was windy, so hair and ceremonial garb were blowing as the crowd waited. Finally, the casket of Paul VI came into view: a plain pine box and, on top of it, an open book of the Gospels with its pages fluttering in the breeze. There, atop the simple coffin, was the message: the pastors of the Church are under the Word of God. They are at the service of the Word.

Most prominent among these ordained leaders is the pope, the center around whom are gathered all the bishops—the successors of the apostles. The pope, as bishop of Rome, is the successor of St. Peter because Peter was the first leader of the church in Rome and there laid down his life for his sheep in martyrdom.

The apostle Peter was originally named Simon. Jesus changed his name with a word play on the Greek word *petros*, meaning "rock": "You are Peter, and on this rock I will build my Church" (Matthew 16:18; see also John 1:42).[6] In the Bible, a name change indicates a special destiny, and, after this incident, we find that Peter does have a central place. At Pentecost, for example, who but Peter speaks for all the apostles?

Peter is imperfect, as are all the apostles, and Jesus certainly knows this. In fact, he even predicts that Peter will deny him! At the same time, Jesus promises his special help. "I have prayed for you that your faith may not fail," he tells Peter, "and when you have turned again, strengthen your brethren" (Luke 22:32). This is Peter's role. Strengthened by Jesus, he strengthens the other apostles and helps maintain their unity. He serves us all by using his authority to bring us to the kingdom. As one of his titles puts it, the pope is truly "the servant of the servants of God."

The Body of Christ

Families and nations are held together by strong bonds indeed. But, in several of his letters, St. Paul uses an even more striking image for the Church that makes clear that its members are united to one another in a deeper, even organic, way. He explains that believers are all "baptized into one body" (1 Corinthians 12:13) and are, therefore, one body in Christ. This means that we are interdependent and interconnected in such a profound way that we are inseparable from one another. To leave the Church would be an amputation, wounding the body and leaving the severed member to wither and die.

As if this were not startling enough, St. Paul goes on to say that this body that is the Church is actually the very body of Christ, who is its head. Perhaps this revelation was given to Paul as he meditated on his own conversion. He was in the process of hunting down *Christians*, but the risen Lord asked him, "Saul, Saul, why do you persecute *me*?" (Acts 9:4; emphasis added). Perhaps Paul knew the story of Jesus' teaching on the Last Judgment, passed down in the Gospel of Matthew, where Jesus pointed out that "as you did it to one of the least of these my brethren, you did it to *me*" (Matthew 25:40; emphasis added).

This reality of the Church as the body of Christ means that Christ, the head, is inseparable from the Church, his body. The lifeblood of Christ is what courses through the veins of this body, sustaining each member. To separate from the body would be to separate oneself from Christ—spiritual suicide. Plus, if the Church is Christ's body, it would make absolutely no sense to love Jesus and despise the Church.

The body of Christ image also helps to correct the view of the Church as a static, hierarchical institution where the clergy do everything and the people just attend. Wherever this impression came from, it is not what the Catholic Church has ever taught about itself. Ordained clergy play a key role. But for the Church to function, every member of the body must play his or her part. Each has a role. Each member is needed.

Communion

Before his death, Jesus said: "And I, when I am lifted up from the earth, will draw all men to myself" (John 12:32). In drawing all to himself, he has drawn us together as a family, a nation, and even as one body. Life is about communion—with God and with our fellow human beings. This vertical and horizontal dimension (communion with God and one another, respectively) finds its supreme expression in the Holy Eucharist, whereby we become one body with Christ and with the Church (see CCC 737 and 1325). You are what you eat, so the saying goes. Christ has given us his sacramental body in order that we may truly become what we receive—his body. As the *Catechism of the Catholic Church* notes, "*The Eucharist makes the Church*" (CCC 1396).

Life is a journey and pilgrimage to the heart of the Father; we return to the Father through the Son and in the Spirit. It is a journey that we take together as a family and a people, one body in Christ. For the Church, as the body of Christ, is the prolongation of the Son's life into time through the Spirit.

Thus, when it comes to the nature of the Church, we should not think primarily of buildings or even hierarchy, still less of bureaucracy. We should think first in terms of *communion*—with Jesus and one another. This is principally established *sacramentally*, in our Baptism and, especially, in the Holy Eucharist. The Church's hierarchy, in its administration of the sacraments and guarding of the truth, is always at the service of this communion.

This communion should naturally lead to a community way of life in the Church that causes people to sit up and take notice. "For by one Spirit we were all baptized into one body. ... If one member suffers, *all suffer together*; if one member is honored, *all rejoice together*" (1 Corinthians 12:13, 26; emphasis added). Evidently, this was lived out in such an intense way during the pagan Roman empire that many pagan Romans, seeing the way Christians related to one another, remarked, "See how they love one another!" [7]

Regrettably, there are probably not many who would see the same thing if they observed a typical Catholic parish today. But making this sacramental communion visible in a new way of life is a task entrusted to all. The holiest, most gifted clergy cannot make it happen by themselves, and the worst cannot stop it from happening. This new way of life, lived in communion, can and should become visible in Christian marriages, families, friendships, ministries, and fellowship groups, even if it is not always apparent on the parish level.

When we find the experience of community lacking in our own local church, it is important to remember that the Church as the family of faith unites the people of God not just in the present but throughout time. In Jesus' resurrection and ascension, the confines of death, time, and space have been overcome. In the Church, the heroes and heroines of the past meet us in the present as our older brothers and sisters. The mystery of the communion of saints can offer us comfort, companionship, and encouragement as we work to make our domestic churches and parishes the vital and intimate communities of faith that they are in their deepest spiritual identity and ought to be in their existential reality.

For this reason, Mordecai's words to Esther apply directly to each one of us; we are here "for such a time as this" (see Esther 4:14). In this age of loneliness and isolation, the Church is called more perfectly and effectively to be the universal sacrament of salvation, a credible sign and effective instrument of unity with God and with one another in Jesus Christ. The Church will not be a wholly and entirely perfect community until every tear is wiped away (see Revelation 21:4) at the end of history. But, until then, we are each called to help make the Church more of what it really is here and now.

And Jesus came and said to them, "*All* authority in heaven and on earth has been given to me. Go therefore and make disciples of *all* nations, baptizing them in the name of the Father and of the Son and of the Holy Spirit, teaching them to observe *all* that I have commanded you; and lo, I am with you *al*ways, to the close of the age."

—Matthew 28:18–20; emphasis added

CHAPTER 2

Our Catholic Heritage

Now that we have gained a little more insight into the Church as the family of God—a holy nation, the body of Christ—we are in a better position to understand what it means to call that Church "Catholic."

Catholic Means *Fullness*

The Greek adjective *katholikos* comes from two Greek words, *kata* and *holos,* literally meaning "according to the whole." It could be translated as comprehensive, whole, full, entire, complete, total, all-embracing, wholistic, even inclusive. Often *catholic* is rendered "universal," in the sense of something that embraces the whole world.

The exact term *katholikos* is not used in the New Testament, but the idea appears everywhere. At Pentecost, people "from every nation under heaven" (Acts 2:5) were added to the Church. In the book of Revelation, John twice saw a vision of people "from every tribe and tongue and people and nation" (Revelation 5:9; see also Revelation 7:9). St. Ignatius of Antioch, whose letter to the Smyrnaeans (about AD 110) provides us with the earliest surviving use of the term, uses "catholic" Church to mean the whole, universal body of Christ as distinguished from simply the "local" church of Smyrna.

Ever since then, the Church founded by Jesus Christ has been called "catholic," or universal, because it is a gathering of all nations in an ever-expanding family of God. But the Church is also fully "catholic" from the very beginning in terms of having received the fullness of truth and life from her Lord.

Being "catholic," then, is also to welcome, conserve, and share the fullness of what Christ gave us—the entire family inheritance. It is to be committed to what St. Paul calls "the whole counsel of God" (Acts 20:27). To be Catholic, in other words, is to be "Christian" without leaving anything out.

To tell the truth, these two meanings of "catholic" are related: it is because the Church has received this fullness from her head, Jesus Christ—the fullness of life, the fullness of truth, the fullness of communion with God—that it has a missionary mandate to all nations (see CCC 831). The Church is bound to share what it has received because it does not exist for its own sake. Rather, it exists to spread this loving communion with the Father through the Son and in the Spirit (see CCC 775–776), even to "the ends of the earth" (Psalm 22:27).[8]

"Heretical" is the polar opposite of "catholic." The term comes from the Greek word meaning choice. Heresy is all about picking and choosing. It is a kind of partiality that often results in the formation of a party, a small sect that appeals to a particular group or a certain type of people. "Catholic" Christianity, on the other hand, seeks to safeguard the truth whole and entire. It cannot restrict itself to any one people or culture. The Catholic Church can never be just one denomination among many. It must embrace all and welcome all. Catholicity, then, is the original and authentic form of inclusiveness.

Catholicity is not, however, the chic, cosmopolitan inclusiveness popular today. The modern world promotes an inclusiveness based on relativism. Everyone can choose his or her own truth and then simply coexist. Such an approach provides no authentic basis for unity but leads instead to a hodge-podge of conflicting parties in a fragile truce. True catholicity is a unity in the truth—the whole truth.

Furthermore, the Church could not be Catholic if God were not Catholic. The Father, in his all-encompassing plan of salvation, gives all that he has to the Son, who, in stretching out his arms on the Cross, embraces the whole world. The Son then entrusts to his Church all that he has received from his Father—his Body, his Blood, his righteousness, his sonship, his mother. All is summed up and contained in his Spirit, the ultimate gift, who opens up to us the unfathomable treasury of grace.

Jesus' last words in the Gospel of Matthew, known as the Great Commission, include the full range of meanings of the term "catholic." Notice how many times the word or particle "all" occurs:

> And Jesus came and said to them, "*All* authority in heaven and on earth has been given to me. Go therefore and make disciples of *all* nations, baptizing them in the name of the Father and of the Son and of the Holy Spirit, teaching them to observe *all* that I have commanded you; and behold, I am with you *al*ways, to the close of the age."
>
> —Matthew 28:18–20; emphasis added

Since the Church is the body of the Risen Lord, who possesses the fullness of truth, authority, and life, St. Paul can go so far as to call the Church "the fulness of him who fills all in all" (Ephesians 1:23). Insofar as the Church is entrusted with the *full* inheritance for the sake of the *whole* world, it can be nothing other than *catholic.*

Tradition and the Fullness of Truth

How is this fullness of truth and life passed from one person to another and from one generation to another? You might answer, "the Bible!" and you would be right—but that is not the whole story.

Jesus' public ministry lasted about three years, and yet he left no writings. For the first twenty years after his resurrection, none of the documents we find in the New Testament had yet been written. So how was the inheritance passed on before there were New Testament Scriptures?

It was by means of Tradition.

When people hear the word tradition, they may recall Jesus' words about "the tradition of men" (Mark 7:8), which some Pharisees used as excuses to avoid obeying divine commandments. Or they may think of family habits, like eating turkey at Thanksgiving or playing pin the tail on the donkey at children's parties. Some may think of something outdated and dusty, lacking in contemporary relevance, like dressing up to go into town. Or, perhaps more positively, they might think nostalgically of something they were fond of once that has little real bearing on their lives now, like handwritten letters. In any case, "tradition" is often seen as something old and, if not dead, barely alive, not much more than an irrelevant relic of the past.

But, for the Catholic Church, Sacred Tradition is not an obsolete holdover from the Dark Ages. It is instead the living transmission of faith and life originating with Jesus, passed on to the apostles and from the apostles to their disciples. The whole process is guided by the Holy Spirit and preserved in the family of God, the Church, down to the present day. One of the most important vehicles for the transmission of this Tradition is the liturgy, which will be discussed further in Part III of this book. Important witnesses to this apostolic tradition are the early Church Fathers, who wrote in the centuries following the apostles, and the Doctors of the Church, whose lives and writings both are exemplary of the Catholic spirit.[9]

Tradition: More Caught than Taught

As we know well from our own experience of family, typically more is caught than is taught. So, too, with the years of our Lord's ministry, the disciples received not only his explicit instruction but were immersed in his very life. They picked up things by osmosis that they never could have learned simply by reading written instructions.

To understand Tradition, it is worth looking at what it meant to be a disciple at the time of Jesus. The Greek word for disciple, *mathetes*, literally means "student"—but not in the modern sense. Typically, at that time, a student would seek out a rabbi and ask to become his disciple. (Hence, it is unique that Jesus called his own disciples.) In contrast to professors and students in the modern university, the ancient rabbi-student relationship was not merely a matter of attending a few lectures. Rather, ancient Jewish students would virtually *live* with their teacher, observing how he prayed, how he served—all in addition to what he formally taught. Being a disciple was more like being an apprentice with a master than a student with a teacher. Disciples picked up from the rabbi things you cannot easily put into words—attitudes and ways of looking at things. Along with his explicit teaching, they picked up these other things implicitly and subconsciously.

When I explain this to my students (Andrew Swafford), I typically observe that once they have had the same professor three or four times, they can often finish his or her sentences! They chuckle because they know it is true. Then I ask them to imagine traveling the country with their favorite professor, watching him or her give the same intro lecture over and over again but also observing how he or she answers questions from the audience and how he or she relates to servers at restaurants and to the people on the hotel staff. Over the course of this extended travel together, suppose such students also meet with their professor regularly behind the scenes and discuss the implications of this teaching and these actions, talking about it, praying over it, and mulling over what it means for their lives.

Imagine further that these modern-day student-disciples were also being coached by this professor to reach out to other people, actively delivering this teaching themselves—all the while continuing to observe their teacher, learning from him or her, and fully receiving this newfound way of life.

Do you think that after all this time—after all this exposure to their teacher and even delivering this teaching themselves—these modern-day student-disciples would remember something of their professor's life and teaching and be able to pass it on? *Of course they would!*

Tradition and Scripture

This gives us some idea of how Sacred Tradition operates and why it is indispensable: Tradition is not merely about intellectual instruction or private lectures that did not make it into the Bible. Rather, Sacred Tradition conveys more than can be written down or put into words—even the inspired words of Scripture. It imparts to us attitudes, assumptions, and an entire frame of reference that formed the original context of the New Testament writings.[10]

Both the writers and the original audience of Scripture stood in the living stream of Tradition. For this reason, the way to read the Bible—which has always been a *communal* book—is to do so from *within* this same living river that formed the Bible's original context.

So the Word of God in all its fullness was passed on first by Tradition and then by Scripture together with Tradition. In fact, this Sacred Tradition literally carries the text to us, even to the present day. So to separate Scripture from Tradition[11] is simply impossible without doing harm to the integrity of the Word of God.

Guarding, preserving, and cherishing this sacred treasure was of first importance to the earliest Christians. St. Paul makes clear here that he saw no opposition between the two ways the Word of God is passed down, orally and in writing: "So then, brethren, stand firm and hold to the *traditions* which you were taught by us, either by word of mouth or by letter" (2 Thessalonians 2:15; emphasis added).

The *Catechism*, quoting the Second Vatican Council, explains the mystery of Sacred Tradition this way: "Through Tradition, 'the Church, in her doctrine, life, and worship perpetuates and transmits to every generation *all* that she herself is, *all* that she believes.'"[12] So Tradition has the power to convey the fullness of the Catholic Faith, *all* that the Lord has received from the Father and handed on to us.

When the apostles (and their close associates) formally set out to write the documents of the New Testament, they wrote to churches that had already received this way of life—churches that were already celebrating the sacraments and passing on this Sacred Tradition within the family of God, the Church.[13] When these churches received various writings of Sacred Scripture, they were read publicly in the context of the liturgy.

So it is the liturgy that is ultimately the privileged custodian and chief vehicle of Sacred Tradition, where the Word of God is proclaimed in preparation for receiving the Word made flesh in the Holy Eucharist.[14] The Church's liturgy—in her prayers, biblical readings, and sacramental rites—expresses this supernatural faith and life given her by the risen Jesus Christ. Along with the Scriptures themselves, the liturgy is among the greatest gifts that Tradition conveys to us.

In the liturgy, time and eternity kiss; in the sacraments, *salvation history is made present*, enabling us to enter the story.[15] In this way, the story of the Bible becomes not a dead letter about the past, but a living story in which we have a part to play. It is indeed *our* story.

Tradition and Traditions

The *Catechism* makes an important distinction between apostolic Tradition (singular) and ecclesiastical traditions. Tradition, with a capital T, is the apostolic *Tradition*, originating with Christ and, therefore, normative for all ages. This Tradition can be identified because it is found always, everywhere, and observed by everyone, to borrow a classic phrase from Vincent of Lerins.[16] For example, the Eucharist is a sacrificial meal that conveys to us Christ's Body and Blood under the appearances of bread and wine. This comes from Christ and was passed on to his apostles, and it has been a constant everywhere in the Catholic world. Hence, it is a normative Tradition and cannot change.

But this *Tradition* of the Eucharist has always been embodied in particular *ecclesiastical traditions*, with a small "t," that have changed over time and vary from place to place. These traditions, such as the vestments of clergy, kneeling, standing, using leavened or unleavened bread,[17] public penance, and particular prayers like the *Gloria*, have arisen in different times and places. They have changed and can change.

Part of the richness of the Catholic Faith in its fullness is the unity that exists within a legitimate and marvelous diversity. Different religious orders and spiritualities (Benedictine, Franciscan, Dominican, Carmelite) along with different liturgical families (Roman, Byzantine, Maronite) are all instances of the one Tradition coming from Christ and the apostles in a rich variety of distinctive traditions.

But how do we know the difference between apostolic Tradition that cannot change and ecclesiastical traditions that can? Who keeps the legitimate diversity of various traditions and cultures from ripping apart the unity and authenticity of the Tradition?

Tradition and Magisterium

It should be obvious to all that any written text is subject to different interpretations. There must be an interpretive authority that is responsible for judging what is in accord with, for example, a nation's founding documents and what is not.

The same is true of Church Tradition. There can be disputes—and there certainly are—as to what belongs to Tradition (which cannot change) and what is merely a tradition (which can change). The Lord feeds us by the Word of God, which comes to us through Scripture and Tradition, and he provides his Church with an authoritative interpreter for both. We call that the *Magisterium*, which refers to the teaching authority invested in the apostles and their successors, the bishops of the Catholic Church. The successors of the apostles, led by the successor of Peter, the pope, have the final word in judging what is in accord with Scripture. They also are the judges of what is Tradition, which must be retained by all, and those small "t" traditions that often can and should be left by the wayside during times of renewal of the Church.

Who Passes on Tradition?

The successors of the apostles have the ultimate responsibility to guard and conserve the deposit of the faith (the Apostolic Tradition). But the whole Church is involved in passing it on. What was noted earlier about the Tradition needs to be recalled here: it conveys more than can be taught in a classroom a day or two per week. One learns the Catholic Tradition much the same way as one best learns a language: by total immersion. This highlights the essential role of the domestic church. Parents and grandparents have the primary role in passing on the Catholic Tradition to children in the family because they, in most cases, spend vast amounts of time with them over many years. Naturally, children pick up their native tongue by immersion in the life of the family. They can "pick up" the perspective of faith in much the same way.

While the family is the primary place where the Tradition is learned and lived, many ministries can serve families in imparting the Catholic Faith to our children. Catholic schools, parish catechetical programs, camps, sports teams, novitiates, and other Catholic apostolates,[18] where people spend a great deal of time together in an atmosphere of faith, are all places where the living Tradition—the fullness of the Catholic Faith—is passed on.

Tradition and Catholic Identity

In summary, as Catholic Christians, we do not pick and choose elements we personally like from the deposit of the faith (see 1 Timothy 6:20) but instead are committed to faithfully preserving the entire apostolic heritage. We do not receive our inheritance from Scripture alone (*sola Scriptura*), but we are devoted to the Word of God as it is transmitted to us by *both* Scripture *and* Tradition and authentically interpreted by the Church's Magisterium.

One cannot be an authentically Catholic Christian without a sense of indebtedness, an awareness of being an heir of a rich inheritance passed on by those who have gone before us. All Catholics, therefore, bear the responsibility to pass on this Tradition not only to the next generation but to the whole world as well. "You received without pay, give without pay" (Matthew 10:8). "Every one to whom much is given, of him will much be required" (Luke 12:48).

The Unique Role of Scripture

Jesus, as far as we know, wrote nothing—except in the sand (see John 8:6). But his disciples lived, prayed, and learned from him day in and day out for about three years. The apostles evidently did the same thing with their disciples for twenty years before the first New Testament document was written. The passing on or handing over of life and truth is called "tradition."

The Word of God comes to us both through Scripture and Tradition. Yet there is something very unique about Scripture: it is the only collection of writings that we actually call the "Word of God." While many writings of saints, popes, and Doctors of the Church are wonderful expressions of Tradition and are guided by the Holy Spirit, Sacred Scripture is *inspired* by the Holy Spirit. The Holy Spirit is so involved in these and only these writings that we see God as their ultimate origin. He can be said to be their author.

Thus, Scripture has a normative role for all "traditions" that are found in Catholic life.

I felt in my bones that
the universe does
not explain itself.

—*C.S. Lewis*

CHAPTER 3

Faith and Reason

Throughout history, the term *catholic* has most often described the family of God—the Catholic Church. But it also describes what the Church believes—the Catholic Faith. The entire second part of this book will discuss the doctrinal content of that Faith. But before we can discuss the "what" of the Faith, we must discuss the "how." What does it mean to believe?

Believing in God?

When people say that they believe in God, they generally mean that they believe that there exists some sort of supreme being who created the universe. Atheism has been with us from at least the fifth or sixth century BC—but always as very much a minority opinion. Virtually every ancient culture known to us was inherently religious. From bands of hunter-gathers in Borneo to the sophisticated Roman Empire of the first century, religion was woven into the fabric of everyday life and was inseparable from it. Atheism is the anomaly. And today, even after nearly two hundred years of sometimes militant atheist propaganda, the vast majority of people still believe in God. Human beings, it seems, are naturally religious beings. What are the roots of this, the sources of our belief in God?[19]

The Cause of the Universe

First, we need to think about the universe in terms of some commonsense principles that we use every day. One of the assumptions that we base our lives on is this: There is an explanation for everything. If there is an effect, there has to be a cause. My parents caused me, their parents caused them, and so on. In this chain of causes, all causes have something in common: each cause is caused by something else. All are bound together as links in a chain.

What if you came across a chain dangling from the sky? Your natural assumption would be that the top of the chain is attached to something stable that anchors the chain and holds it in place. If I were to tell you that there was no such thing, only endless links in the chain, you would shake your head and say it was impossible.

That is what a universe like ours would be—like a chain dangling in space—if its causes and effects were not anchored to something unchanging, stable, and firm. Unlike all the effects that depend on a prior cause, this stable and firm reality is not an effect but has always existed. Nothing came before it. It is an uncaused cause, the unmoved mover that puts in motion all the other causes that ultimately result in you and me.

Creation implies a creator. This is common sense. It has been understood intuitively by most people from the beginning of time and is one reason why most people throughout history have believed in God.[20]

Let us look at a similar self-evident truth. A design implies the existence of a designer. When we see the neatly clipped shrubbery, glorious flowerbeds, and manicured lawn of the palace gardens of Versailles, we wonder who the master gardener is. Left to themselves, things tend not to become more orderly but to deteriorate and lapse into disorder. A garden left to itself does not remain a garden very long. When we hear a symphony, we wonder who the composer might be. We know that if all the performers of all the instruments just played random notes to a random rhythm, the result would not be Beethoven's Fifth.

Now the universe exhibits a much more elaborate design than a palace garden or a symphony. And the more we learn about life, from the human brain to the recently mapped code of human DNA, the more we uncover a design so intricate, so perfect, that it boggles the mind.[21]

No one would suppose that the code of a Windows or macOS operating system had written itself or simply resulted from chance. But the instructions that appear "programmed into" DNA are many times more complex than the system software written by great coding geniuses. Common sense says that such brilliant design could only be the work of an intelligent designer—in other words, God.

You do not need a degree in philosophy or science to figure this out. A great deal of slick and complicated arguments are required to wiggle out of this intuitive and common-sense perception. C.S. Lewis was certainly a towering intellect, which most of us are not. Yet we can easily relate to what he says here about why he, formerly a "sophisticated" atheist, came to the conviction that God exists: "I felt in my bones that the universe does not explain itself."[22]

The Desires of the Human Heart and Conscience

When we look at the human person, we notice a few more striking things that point to an infinite creator. People are not usually content with just having enough material things for survival or even for relative comfort. There is an insatiable desire in the human heart for something more. Nothing like this can be observed in other creatures.

Some people try to satisfy this desire with more money, sex, work, or power. But the desire for "something more" remains. Many people experience it as persistent emptiness. If nothing in this world satisfies us, the desire itself might be evidence that the source of our happiness is not to be found in this created world at all. If our desire is infinite, only something infinite will satisfy it. But if nothing infinite exists to satisfy our infinite desire, then our human existence is little more than a tragic riddle.

Infinite truth, goodness, and beauty are other names for God. St. Augustine put it well. Addressing God, from whom he had run for some thirty years, Augustine observed truthfully, "Our hearts are restless until they rest in you."[23]

Something else about human beings also points beyond this world. We have, deep in our souls, a voice that commands us to do good and avoid evil. We call this the voice of conscience. Those who want to obey this voice seek to understand the good they must do and the evil they must avoid. Some get it wrong. Others try to silence this troubling voice that makes such absolute claims. Still others deny the existence of moral obligations yet acknowledge them implicitly when they object to unfairness or lying or violence. The reality is that we are all aware to some degree that we—and our neighbors—must be just and truthful, even though we might argue about what justice or truth means in this or that circumstance.

Where does this voice of conscience come from? Only an absolute lawgiver could make an absolute claim on our behavior like this. Conscience is the voice of God.[24]

Proofs?

These sources of our belief in God are principal arguments for the existence of God. Of the ones we have mentioned here, two are based on observation of the cosmos and two are drawn from reflection on the mystery of the human person. However, there are many more that we will not review here.

Are these arguments strong enough to be considered *proofs*? The answer is yes. But they are not like mathematical proofs. Neither are they scientific proofs. They do not employ the scientific method, using observation, measurements, and experiments. They are proofs based in reason—in reasoning from effects to causes—which is usually the way a prosecutor proves a court case. He or she assembles evidence that together argues, beyond a reasonable doubt, that the defendant committed the crime in question.

Is any one of these arguments sufficient to prove the existence of God? Perhaps. Each one on its own has been accepted as decisive by various seekers throughout history. But when you put all the arguments together, the case for a creator becomes overwhelming. The arguments become, in the words of St. John Henry Newman, a case of converging probabilities.[25]

Interestingly, scientists themselves reason this way in many important circumstances. When the existence of something cannot be directly observed, scientists marshal evidence to show that it exists. For example, certain subatomic particles, quarks, *cannot* be directly observed. Yet scientists are confident of their existence because of the effects that *can* be observed. The same can be said for black holes: We infer their existence from their gravitational effects. The way we reason to God's existence is analogous: From observed effects, we arrive at the unseen cause of those effects, and that unseen cause is God.

Arguments Against God's Existence

What are the arguments *against* the existence of God? They all boil down to two, which St. Thomas Aquinas conveniently identified in the thirteenth century.[26] The first is that the existence of evil and injustice in the world, causing suffering of the innocent, argues against the existence of a good God. And the second is that we can explain the universe and the human person perfectly well without God, thank you very much.

The suffering of the innocent has confounded people throughout human history. The entire biblical book of Job wrestles with this question. God's answer to Job is that man is not God and is not able to comprehend God's designs. In other words, the book of Job teaches us that evil and the suffering of the innocent are not a problem that the human mind can simply solve like a crossword puzzle. They are a mystery to be questioned and probed.

We know that much human suffering results from foolish and evil choices. The omnipotent God could easily prevent this by taking away human freedom, making us like robots programmed to always do good. But he made us for love, and, by its very nature, love must be freely given. If God were to take away our freedom to keep us from doing evil, he would also take away our ability to love. This would be a greater evil than the loss of health or even the loss of life.

Although God permits evil, he never wills it directly. And, in his surpassing wisdom, God finds a way to bring good out of evil. The greatest example of bringing a great good out of monstrous evil is the suffering and death of Jesus, by which death and sin were conquered for all time. Most of us, reflecting on our lives, can discover some evil from which God has brought great good.

The other objection, that we do not need God to explain either the universe or the human person, has been proved by science, hasn't it? Didn't Darwin prove that random natural selection explains all life on earth, dispensing with our need for God?

Not quite. Darwin himself realized that natural selection does not explain the origin of life, and he openly admitted it.[27] Natural selection, popularly referred to as "the survival of the fittest," is a theory that explains much about why certain genetic traits come to predominate in a certain species. But it does not explain how life originates.

Extending the theory of natural selection, some hold that random chance is the governing factor in the development of life. This is a hypothesis, an assumption made for the sake of discussion or further exploration. Many scientists argue that it does not account for the facts we know—and the more facts we discover, the weaker the hypothesis seems. But whether it is a weak or strong hypothesis, it is far from being settled science. It is a useful tool for research, but it is not fact. The problem with it is that, for some, it has become a form of belief.

Additional discoveries may further strengthen the theory of natural selection as an explanation of genetic change and diversity, and stronger hypotheses about the origins of life may be proposed. But neither can explain—science itself cannot explain—why there is something rather than nothing. Why any universe at all? And why this one?

When the Big Bang Theory was first proposed in 1927 (by a scientist who happened to be a Catholic priest), it made many scientists extremely uncomfortable. If it is true, as now is generally accepted, anything that existed before the Big Bang would have been destroyed in that primordial explosion. That means that science will never be able to study it. Science has bumped up against an absolute limit beyond which it may not advance. That moment sounds a lot like the moment of creation in which God said, "Let there be light" (Genesis 1:3).

A NASA scientist commenting on the implications of the Big Bang puts it this way: "For the scientist who has lived by his faith in the power of reason, the story ends like a bad dream. He has scaled the mountain of ignorance; he is about to conquer the highest peak; as he pulls himself over the final rock, he is greeted by a band of theologians who have been sitting there for centuries."[28]

Can We Know More by Reason?

What kind of God is this, the first cause of the universe? From the time of Aristotle in the fourth century BC, philosophers have sought to discern God's attributes. If this being is necessary and uncaused, then he has no beginning and no end. In other words, his power and intelligence are infinite. That means he is eternal, almighty, and all-knowing. And since there cannot be two or more *all*-mighty beings, God the Creator must be one.[29]

These are some of the things one can know about the Creator through reason alone. They are not based on any personal acquaintance with this Unmoved Mover. We get to them simply by observing the effects of his work.

This God of the philosophers is impressive but rather impersonal. One can have cool, controlled classroom discussions about him, but it would be hard to get passionately excited about such a Creator. Deducing that such a God exists is one thing. Getting to know him is something else entirely.

Revelation

This is where *revelation* comes in—that is, God making himself and his ways known to man through his self-revelation. To illustrate the difference between an Unmoved Mover and a God we can know personally through revelation, Louis Bouyer, a French theologian, used Daniel Defoe's famous tale of Robinson Crusoe. Marooned on a desert island, Crusoe believed himself utterly alone. But he noticed something in the sand resembling a human footprint. Then he came across what looked like the remnants of a fire. After several such discoveries, he arrived at the conclusion that someone else was on the island. Not long after, while he was making his way through the jungle, a young man suddenly stepped out of the undergrowth and introduced himself. Crusoe named him Friday for the day of the week on which the encounter took place. The two went on to become inseparable companions, building a life and a friendship together in that desolate place.

In the case of our knowledge of God, no searching or reasoning can take us from acceptance of an Unmoved Mover to love for the living God of Abraham, Isaac, and Jacob. For this to happen, God had to step out of the shadows and reveal himself.

This is precisely what he did, entering human history and making himself known in both words and deeds. Abraham heard an invitation. Jacob had a wrestling match. Moses saw a burning bush. The people of Israel saw the sea open before them. They heard his voice as thunder on the mountain. Through the Law and the prophets, Israel gradually came to know more and more about what he was like, all the while building a relationship with him. Finally, God fully disclosed himself and his wonderful plan through the person, teaching, and redemptive work of Jesus Christ.

This record of God's words and saving work in history is transmitted to each of us through Scripture and Tradition. There are many doctrines about God's inner life and his plan for us that are revealed in the course of salvation history: that God is one in nature but three Persons—Father, Son, and Holy Spirit; that the eternal Son entered history, taking flesh in Jesus of Nazareth; that Jesus was conceived by the Holy Spirit and born of a virgin; that he died for our sins, rose again for our justification, and ascended into glory; that he is both true God and true man; that he sent his Holy Spirit, who gave birth to the Church and makes the sacraments possible; and that Jesus will come again in glory as judge and Savior.

Faith, Reason, and Science

These beliefs, these convictions that we will discuss further in Part II of this book, are essential truths that God wants us to know. Some revealed truths, like the existence of God, can be demonstrated by reason alone, even apart from divine revelation. Other revealed truths—like the Trinity, the Incarnation, and the Virgin Birth—could never have been discovered by the use of reason alone, though all of them are eminently reasonable.

One of the characteristics of the Catholic approach to faith is that faith and reason are seen as two complementary paths to understanding reality. Since there is only one truth, faith and reason and Scripture and science can never be in conflict. If there does seem to be a conflict, it is only apparent. It is either caused by bad theology, as in the Galileo affair,[30] or by an inadequate theory masquerading as settled science. Catholic faith is not threatened by science or philosophy. That is why the Church has always been a patron not only of the arts and philosophy but also of the sciences.[31]

Dogma

As Catholic Christians, we accept revealed truths on the authority of God, who revealed them, and on the testimony of the Church's teaching authority, which attests to this fact. That is what a dogma[32] is—a truth that the Church, vested with its authority by Christ himself, guarantees to have been revealed by God, and is, therefore, to be accepted by faith.[33]

God revealed it. I believe it. That settles it.

But faith involves much, much more than simple intellectual acceptance of revealed truths. When a Catholic professes the creed and says, "I believe in One God . . . ," he or she means much more than these various propositions about him. Here is what St. James says about holding correct beliefs about God: "You believe that God is one; you do well. Even the demons believe— and shudder" (James 2:19).

Let us call right beliefs about God "convictions." The author of Hebrews mentions "the conviction of things not seen" (Hebrews 11:1) as an ingredient of faith. "For whoever would draw near to God must believe that he exists and that he rewards those who seek him" (Hebrews 11:6). Notice here that Hebrews describes these beliefs not as faith in God but as *prerequisite* convictions for those who would "draw near to God." One can be a great distance away from God, as are the demons, and still have correct convictions about him. Without actually taking an additional step, that is precisely where a person would remain—distant from God. In other words, simple belief or conviction does not save. The critical movement from belief or conviction to faith, which does save, is what our next chapter is about.

The Catholic Contribution to Modern Science

Few realize how extensive the Catholic contribution to modern science really is. Contemporary physicist Stephen Barr lists the following clerics (bishops, priests, or religious) as having made important contributions to concepts such as inertia, the rotation of the earth on its axis, the application of mathematics to the physical world, the refraction of light, and even biology—the majority of whose work long precedes Galileo (1564–1642): Robert Grosseteste (ca. 1168–1253); Thomas Bradwardine (1290–1349); Nicholas of Oresme (1323–1382); Nicolas of Cusa (1401–1464); Copernicus (1473–1543); Marin Mersenne (1588–1648); Christoph Scheiner (1573–1650); Francesco Grimaldi (1613–1653); Giovanni Riccioli (1598–1671); Pietro Secchi (1818–1878); Giuseppe Piazzi (1746–1826); Lazzaro Spallanzani (1729–1799).[34] This list is just a small sample of the numerous Catholic clergy who have made significant contributions to modern science over the past millennia.

Jesuit contributions to astronomy are also well known. In addition, we have Gregor Mendel (1822–1884), the Austrian monk and pioneer in genetics, and Fr. Georges Lemaître (1894–1966), who proposed the Big Bang Theory. Barr comments, "Obviously, had the church been hostile to science and reason, or had religious faith been incompatible with the scientific temper of mind, so many ecclesiastical figures would not have been found making major scientific discoveries."[35]

CHAPTER 4

A Journey and a Commitment

Faith can be described as *the* distinctive Christian word. In the New Testament, *pistis,* the Greek word for faith, occurs 243 times. By way of comparison, the word for hope is found only 53 times, and *agape,* the term for divine love, 116 times. It is, therefore, extremely important that we get it right, that we understand all that this term really means. To do that, we need to further examine the purpose of revelation and the original setting for the profession of Catholic Faith: the creed.

Response to Revelation

Religion is humanity's search for God; revelation is God's pursuit of humanity. As the Good Shepherd in Jesus' parable left the ninety-nine to go in search for the one stray (see Luke 15:4), so God comes looking for us to bring us back to himself. He reveals himself not just to get our thoughts straight but to re-establish a loving relationship with us. Lovers reveal themselves to one another. In divine revelation, God discloses himself and takes us into his confidence. By revealing himself, writes theologian Henri de Lubac, "God, so to speak, has laid bare his own inner life by unveiling his designs to us."[36]

The good shepherd knows his sheep and calls each of them by name (see John 10:3–5). And so revelation is always a call, an invitation, a proposal that is addressed not just globally to the people of Israel or to the whole world but intimately and personally, to each of us—Abraham, Jacob, Moses, Paul, you, me. It is an invitation that demands a response. The response can be yes, or it can be no. Saying no can be direct and explicit. Or the invitation can be totally ignored, and the RSVP indefinitely postponed. This is perhaps the most common way of saying no (see Matthew 22:1–14).

The yes to God's invitation to a relationship is what is meant by faith. It is a response not just of the mind to doctrines but of the whole person to a Person—to a God who is so personal that he is a communion of Persons.

Faith as a Journey

We are very used to the phrase to "believe in" God. But one does not really find this construction in the Old Testament, and it was not found in the everyday Greek that was the common language of the Roman Empire when the New Testament was written. It is an expression that appears to have been coined by the early Christian community, perhaps by Jesus himself (see John 14:1). It had to be developed, it seems, to express the distinctive act of Christian faith. It puts together a verb *pisteuein*, meaning "to believe," with a preposition *eis*, which has the dynamic sense of a movement *into* something. The author of Hebrews hints at this movement in a text we have already mentioned in this book: "For whoever would *draw near* to God must believe" (Hebrews 11:6; emphasis added). Believing is faith in the truest sense when it includes this movement toward or into God. Through his self-revelation, God draws near to us. Faith responds by drawing near to him.

Baptism and Creed in the Early Church

What "believing into" means is illustrated dramatically by the baptismal rite of the early Church.[37] On Holy Saturday night, the candidates for Baptism would be assembled. They would face west, where the sun slips into darkness,[38] and would be asked three questions. "Do you renounce Satan?" They would answer "I do." "And all his works?" "I do." "And all his empty promises?" "I do." This clearly is a decree of divorce. It is a renunciation of a prior relationship.

The candidates would then be led into the baptismal pool. Now the questions would continue. "Do you believe in God, the Father Almighty, creator of heaven and earth?" They would answer, "I do." They would then be plunged into and under the water." After emerging, they would be asked, "Do you believe in Jesus Christ, his only Son our Lord ... ?" Once again, "I do" would be followed by an immersion." And finally, "Do you believe in the Holy Spirit ... ?" Another "I do" and another immersion.

Baptism, the sacrament of faith, here graphically illustrates what faith is about: an immersion in the death and resurrection of Christ, a plunge into the triune God. It is a marriage following from the solemn repudiation of a former relationship.

In the fourth century, when the Church could safely construct public buildings for worship, this ceremony often took place in a separate building called a baptistry.[39] The imagery of a wedding surrounded this ceremony. The newly baptized were clothed in white garments. They processed into the church building proper holding candles, in what St. Cyril of Jerusalem called "the nuptial procession," on their way to partake, for the first time, of "the wedding feast of the Lamb."[40]

Faith and Love

When faith and love are distinguished, as St. Paul does in 1 Corinthians 13, it can give the impression that they are two completely different things. But a closer examination of the context of Paul's words reveals that he is speaking here primarily of love of the brothers and sisters. Faith, for him and the other New Testament writers, is not simply correct beliefs about God. To be a truly living, saving faith, it must include at least some degree of love of God.

The fact that love and faith cannot be separated is evident in the wedding imagery for Baptism and by the creed in the early Church. The articles of faith contained in the creed were not recited as if new members of a political party were assenting to various planks of the party platform. Rather, they were proclaimed in the context of making a vow. In fact, the same language was used that we use today in making wedding vows: "I do."

For St. Paul, the act of faith is not an intellectual act alone. For him, we believe not so much with the mind as with the heart (see Romans 10:10). This means we believe not just with our emotions but from the very center or core of our being, which includes all of our faculties, intellect, will, emotions, and soul.

The English word "core" comes from *cor*, the Latin word for heart. To believe, *credere* in Latin, is to give one's heart (*cor* + *dare*, the Latin verb "to give"). Even in the English language the verb "be-*lieve*" comes from an ancient Germanic term meaning to cherish or *love*.

To believe in God is to adhere to him, to cling to him, to latch on to him as a child latches on to his or her mother's breast, to attach and abide in him as a grafted branch abides in the vine (see John 15).

We often talk about Christianity as a body of doctrine. Here, we must recall that if beliefs are faith's body, love is faith's soul. A body without a soul is a cadaver. The soul is the "form" of the body, using classic theological terminology. This is why Catholic Tradition calls right beliefs devoid of charity "unformed faith."[41] St. James calls such faith "dead."

Standing: the Posture of Confidence

Everywhere, in both the Old and New Testaments, there are two related postures that are associated with faith.

The first is standing.

One of the most common words in religious language is the Hebrew term *amen*. Often it is explained as meaning "so be it." It is true that it is used this way at times in Jewish and Christian culture. But this is not its original or primary meaning. *Amen* comes from the word for "firm," and the image that goes along with it is a rock. To say "amen" to God's truth is to say that it is rock solid, that I can and will stand on it. I will even stake my life on it.

In winter, bodies of water often freeze. Faith is not just having an opinion that the ice is thick enough for a hockey game. Faith is stepping onto the ice, trusting that it is firm enough to support one's weight. Faith, as it were, entrusts itself to the ice.

True faith must include this element of vulnerability and self-involvement. Faith takes risks. It includes confidence or trust. This trust that stands on the promises of God is the predominant characteristic of faith as extolled in the psalms.

The Darkness of Faith

Since God's revelation is reasonable, faith is not completely blind. It sees but just not clearly or completely. Pope Francis, in *Lumen Fidei* (2013), his encyclical on faith, says that faith is a light. But it is more like an oil lamp (see Psalm 119:105) than like the brilliant light of the sun. In the time of Jesus, an oil lamp was generally small enough to fit in the palm of one's hand. It obviously could not emit much light, just enough to see dimly within a few feet around the lamp.

St. Paul contrasts the knowledge we have by faith to the clear vision we will have in heavenly glory: "Now we see in a mirror dimly, but then face to face" (1 Corinthians 13:12). A first-century mirror was not like the glass-covered mirrors we have today, which provide a very sharp and clear image. They were instead simply a sheet of metal. The hazy, fuzzy image you see of yourself when you look at your reflection in a stainless-steel refrigerator is what Paul is referring to as the kind of obscure knowledge we have now by faith.

Looking at a pond after a winter freeze, you *can* see the frozen surface, but you *cannot* see how thick it is. If God says step out in faith, you may find yourself tending to hesitate. Trust is required. To St. Peter's credit, when the Lord invited Peter to walk to him on the water, Peter stepped out of the boat (see Matthew 14:29). This is a poignant image of the *confidence* required by faith.

Faith as a Free Act

To entrust oneself to God or to one's spouse is a free act of self-giving. If all could be seen clearly, no trust would be required and there would be no real choice in the matter. God provides evidence for faith, sometimes miracles, and other times rational arguments that support the reasonableness of faith. Yet these assurances, called "motives of credibility," are never given by God in such an overwhelming way as to compel belief. In heaven, when we see "face to face" with complete, unclouded vision, the beauty and goodness of God will be so compelling that there will be no way we can refuse it.

But God made us for love. And love involves a *free* act of self-giving, a *choice* to entrust oneself to another. He wants our love, not simply our forced obedience. He will, therefore, not violate our freedom. Only after we make our free choice and walk the rest of our life in fidelity to that choice will we be given the overwhelming experience of seeing him face to face.

Walking: the Posture of Commitment

The second posture associated with faith is walking.

Interestingly, the small oil lamps of the ancient world could be fastened to one's sandals. Since such lamps contained but a few drops of oil, you could walk with them attached. As such, they served as the biblical equivalents of a flashlight. Naturally, you could only see far enough to take the next step in your journey. But every step you took meant you could see where to put your feet next as you made your way toward your destination.

No wonder that St. Paul uses "walking" as a metaphor for another necessary dimension of saving faith—the willingness to act on God's commands. "We walk by faith, not by sight" (2 Corinthians 5:7). Paul also speaks of "the obedience of faith" (Romans 1:5; 16:26). The radical commitment of Baptism entails a whole new way of life. Faith includes the *commitment* to embark on this new way of life, one step at a time. The believer may stumble and fall because of inexperience, weakness, or uneven ground, but committed faith just gets up and keeps walking.

Scripture provides us with many powerful models of faith who have kept on walking. Abraham's whole life was walking in obedience and trust—from Mesopotamia to Canaan and to the summit of Mount Moriah (see Genesis 12, 22). Mary's fiat was followed by a hundred-mile walk to visit her cousin Elizabeth. How could she be sure that her barren, aged cousin was pregnant? All she had was the Word of God delivered by an angel. As for Joseph, not a word of his is recorded in the Gospels. But we are told that, in response to God's Word, delivered to him in a sequence of dreams, he walked a hundred miles to Bethlehem, two hundred miles further to Egypt, and another three hundred miles back to Nazareth. In this, Joseph, the just man, is one of the greatest biblical models of the "obedience of faith"—faith as commitment.

Faith, Works, Growth

When faith is understood in its fullness and integrity, including conviction, confidence, and commitment, it becomes apparent that faith and works go hand in hand; they are both indispensable aspects of being a faithful Christian.

Jesus said, "No one can come to me unless the Father who sent me draws him" (John 6:44). God seeks us. He draws us to himself. The Father sends the Holy Spirit to attract us to Christ, enabling us to take our first steps of faith.

Our forgiveness and the possibility of a relationship with God, what St. Paul calls "justification," is God's free gift to us. This is what *grace* means. It is not something we can earn by anything we do. Even the act of faith, our yes to this gift, is itself a gift. But the faith cannot be forced. It is a gift we can accept or reject. We have the freedom to say yes, and we also have the freedom to resist, harden our hearts, and say no.

But our acceptance of God's forgiveness, our yes to his offer of grace, involves a willingness to walk in the way of his commandments. It is not either faith *or* works that pleases God. It is faith *that* works. Faith that refuses to work is a faith without legs, a faith without soul. That is why St. James says that such "faith" is dead (see James 2:17–18).

There is yet another conclusion to draw from the image of faith as walking. Living faith is a perpetual journey. Nourished by Word and sacrament and exercised by walking, faith develops. It is not a one-time acceptance of doctrines to be professed. Neither is it a one-time acceptance of Jesus Christ as one's personal Savior, whether at the time of Baptism or in a moment of personal conversion. It is a never-ending adventure of growth and development. Faith is not simply passive belief or even passive trust in God but rather a life-long, avid pursuit of him.

PART II

Our Faith

If you understood him,
it would not be God.

— *St. Augustine*

CHAPTER 5

One God, the Father Almighty

At the heart of the Catholic Faith is the creed. We profess many doctrines, but they all boil down to a single object of our Faith—the mystery of God and his saving plan for us.

The creed is a kind of condensed version of Catholic doctrine. In the Church's early days, new believers were asked a series of questions before they were baptized. Do you believe in God? Do you believe that Jesus Christ rose from the dead? Do you believe in the Holy Spirit? In the communion of saints? The early creeds arose from these questions and their answers.

The wording of the early creeds thus varied somewhat from city to city. The version we know now as the Apostles' Creed was basically the baptismal profession of the church in Rome. The longer Nicene Creed was the baptismal creed of Nicaea, a city in the Eastern Roman Empire. Two Church councils later developed the Nicene Creed further to clarify the Church's faith in the face of several dangerous heresies.

The basic form of the creed arises from the Great Commission, when Jesus commanded his disciples to baptize "in the name of the Father and of the Son and of the Holy Spirit" (Matthew 28:19). The creed consists of a threefold structure because it is a baptismal pledge of loyalty and commitment to the three Persons of the Holy Trinity.

The Creed: the Symbol of Faith

While the creed is a profession of faith, it is also a *symbolon*, a symbol of faith. In the same way that a wedding band is a sign and token of the vows that a husband and wife exchange in Matrimony, the creed is a sign of the nuptial covenant we make as Christians with the Triune God.

The New Testament describes the Church as the Bride of Christ (see Ephesians 5:32; Revelation 22:17), and that is what we are. The creed is the wedding band of faith,[42] and, like a wedding band, it is a sign by which we recognize one another as Christians, that is, as members of the bridal community of the Church.

For a marriage to be legitimate, it requires the informed consent of both husband and wife, for the pledge of one's heart and one's life has to be made freely, with full knowledge of the person to whom it is made. Since many erroneous ideas about the identity and character of God were circulating in the days of the early Church, it was necessary to include in the creed clarifying descriptions of God and his work as part of the baptismal vows.

We must emphasize again that the object of the Church's Faith is not *something* but *someone*: the Triune God. So here, in Part II of this book, we will examine our Catholic faith by following the general threefold structure of the creed, which describes in turn each Person of the Trinity—the Father, the Son, and the Holy Spirit.

Talking About God

We mentioned earlier that whenever we speak of God and his works, we are beyond our depth, out of our league, because the human mind is finite while God is infinite. It is common sense that something finite cannot possibly contain what is infinite. Therefore, as St. Augustine points out, "If you understood him, it would not be God."[43] This echoes what Job said: "God is great, and we know him not."[44]

This does not mean that there is nothing that we can understand about God. It means that there is so much to understand that our finite minds can never fully contain it all. God can be approached, but he cannot be mastered. His mystery can be pondered but not solved like a math problem. The good news is that we can never become bored with God. The more acquainted we become with him, the more there is to discover and the greater our desire to discover it.[45]

God wants us not simply to obey him but to know him. He has given us reason by which we can know some things about him. He has also given us revelation by which we can become much more sure of what we know about him, and, more importantly, we can become familiar with him. He has revealed himself to us through both words and deeds, as we have seen.

Now, however, it is time to note that there are two primary ways to understand God. First is the negative way (*via negativa*). Here, we eliminate false possibilities by being absolutely clear about what God is *not* like. When we call him "infinite," for example, we are basically doing this. We are saying he is *not* limited as all created things are. This approach is a safe way to go. But to restrict ourselves to this approach exclusively would be too confining.

God wants us to go further than this. He wants us to know something of what he is actually like. So he comes down to our level and reveals himself through images, symbols, and analogies drawn from our human experience. Psalm 118 says, "The right hand of the LORD has struck with power" (*Lectionary*: 446). This conveys in a beautiful way a sudden, mighty, and decisive intervention by God in our history. God uses human language and concepts to communicate with us, but this anthropomorphic language does not mean that God is human as we are. God is spirit and does not literally have a right arm (see John 4:24).

This may seem so obvious that it need not be said. But human beings have a funny way of forgetting it. Sometimes people push a biblical analogy so far that it results in a distorted image of God and his work. So, as we begin our discussion of the creed, we recall that all analogies that we use when describing God, even those analogies given to us by Sacred Scripture, are inadequate. We must approach God and his plan with modesty, humility, and awe. Like Moses before the mystery of the burning bush, we must "take off our shoes," for we are standing on holy ground.

One God

The first statement of the Nicene Creed is "I believe in one God." When this creed was first professed, Christians lived in a polytheistic world. Jews were the outliers, a peculiar people with the seemingly strange notion that only one God existed. Jews actually made the confession of God's oneness during a daily ritual, and, even in our own day, faithful Jewish men[46] proclaim every morning and evening, "Hear, O Israel: the LORD our God is one LORD" (Deuteronomy 6:4).

All the commandments of God, including the Ten Commandments, flow from this reality that God is one. So the first commandment on Sinai was "You shall have no other gods before me" (Exodus 20:3). The greatest commandment in Deuteronomy adds a positive to this negative. Since there is only one God, "You shall love the LORD your God with *all* your heart, and with *all* your soul, and with *all* your might" (Deuteronomy 6:5; emphasis added).

The oneness of God demands that we worship him alone. This brings focus and coherence to our lives. It unifies our lives around a center that is truly the center of all reality. And it provides a unifying foundation for all people throughout the world.

Idolatry is about worshipping something other than God. Idols are, in fact, often made according to the idol-maker's image and likeness. If you examine the Roman pantheon, for example, you can easily see this. Jupiter, Juno, Mars, Venus, and the other "gods" have all the foibles and passions that we have, only on a much larger, even titanic scale.

One idol usually does not satisfy for long, so another is made. Idolatry thus leads to polytheism, a confused pantheon of different gods who are often in conflict. In the story of the Trojan war told in the *Iliad*, for example, some gods are sponsoring one army, while different gods support the other army. This illustrates how polytheism leads not to unity but to dissolution and dissipation both in the human heart and in human society.[47]

The great *Shema* of Israel, the call to confess and worship the one God and that God alone, is the first thing to be mentioned in the creed.

A Personal, Transcendent God

Some atheists of the nineteenth and twentieth centuries leveled the charge that the God of the Bible was just another projection of humanity, made in man's image and likeness. They alleged that the religion of the Bible was just as childish as that of the Greeks and Romans.

As scientific discoveries proliferated during these centuries and awareness of powerful forces of nature increased, the idea became more popular that the Creator is an impersonal force standing at the origin of the universe, holding it all together. This has been popularized in many ways, including the Star Wars franchise with its greeting "May the Force be with you."

Some identify this force with "energy" or with the universe as a whole. For these persons, "spirituality" is simply awareness of our oneness with this force, this energy, this universal soul. After death, our personalities will just dissolve and merge back into this powerful but impersonal life-force.

The name for this belief is *pantheism,* from a Greek expression meaning that everything equals god. Some people think such a conception is more sophisticated and scientific than the traditional idea of a personal God. But pantheism is not as reasonable as it sounds. The highest order of being that we know of is personal being. *Person* implies self-consciousness, intellect, and will. In other words, a personal being is truly free. An impersonal force lacks these things. It may be powerful, like gravity, but, if it lacks intellect, will, and, therefore, freedom, it is actually less perfect than we are, not more. God is, by definition, the supreme being. He must, then, be *more* personal than we are, not *less.*

If he is the Creator, he cannot be simply the sum of all created things. He must be uncreated and infinitely superior to all that he has created, not identical with it. The image of heaven is a way of getting this across—that God is transcendent, of a higher order, the most-high, far surpassing all created things. The Christian philosopher Søren Kierkegaard was fond of putting it this way: There is an infinite qualitative difference between us and God.[48]

Trinity

So, if Catholics believe in one God, how can we confess that God is three Persons?

Reason could not have arrived at this. Neither could human imagination have devised it. The reason Christians believe it is because God, taking us into his confidence, has revealed it to us as the secret of his inner life. At Jesus' baptism, the Trinity was made manifest by way of the Father's voice from heaven, the beloved Son in the water, and the Spirit descending upon the Son. Jesus' very instructions at the end of the Matthew's Gospel imply it: ". . . baptizing them in the name [not names] of the Father and of the Son and of the Holy Spirit" (Matthew 28:19). One name, one being, one substance, one God—three Persons.

The word *trinity*, like the word *catholic*, is not found in the New Testament. The term was coined somewhat simultaneously in the late second century by one father of the Church writing in Greek and another writing in Latin.[49] The term is simply a very handy way to refer to the reality found explicitly throughout the New Testament and implicitly in the Old.[50]

So God is not just personal. He is interpersonal. St. John's affirmation that "God is love" (1 John 4:16) now takes on greater meaning. God was not a solitary monarch before he brought creatures into being. From all eternity, God is a communion of Persons who are ceaselessly giving themselves to one another in love. The foundation of all being is not the atom or some blind force but the force of the eternal love of the Father, Son, and Holy Spirit.

God the Father

Calling the first Person of this Trinity "Father" cannot, then, be limited to his fatherly care of his creatures. Otherwise, God would have only become "Father" at the moment of creation. No, God is always and eternally who he is. There is no change in God (see James 1:17). God is eternally Father, or he is not a father at all.

Knowing that no words are adequate to express this mystery, let us at least try to gain some insight into it.

From all eternity, God loves. He speaks his love and begets it—his Word, his Son. We call the Word "the only begotten Son of God," but his begetting is eternal: The Son receives his being from the Father not in one moment but in every moment. The Son, thus, possesses the fullness of God's nature for all time—his divine substance with all his divine attributes.

The Father loves the Son perfectly, giving himself completely to his Son. And the Son loves the Father perfectly, giving all of himself in return to his Father. This bond of love is so real that it has its own reality, a Personhood distinct from the Father and the Son. This uncreated and eternal love—of the Father for the Son and of the Son for the Father—we call the Holy Spirit.

And so we believe in the Father, the Son, and the Holy Spirit—three Persons, one God, one divine substance. Each divine Person is fully God, and yet each Person is distinct from the others. I wish we could say more here. But, however much we write, it could never be sufficient to capture the fullness of the beauty and splendor of the divine mystery of God as an eternal communion of love.

Father of Mercy

Many smirk at the image of God the Father as an old man with a beard. The Father is not a male human being, true. God the Father transcends male and female: He is pure spirit and, therefore, has no corporal body (see CCC 239).

But the image of God the Father by Michelangelo on the ceiling of the Sistine Chapel does convey a great deal. While he holds Eve tenderly, close to his heart, he is reaching out his finger to give life to Adam.

This painting vividly portrays Deuteronomy's image of God who, like a loving father, carries his child Israel along on the way (see Deuteronomy 1:31). It conveys one of the main meanings of the fatherhood of God: that he is not only the origin of all being, possessing transcendent authority, but he has the compassion and tenderness of a father for his children (see Psalm 103:13). He is, as St. Paul says, the "Father of mercies"[51] and "God of all comfort" (2 Corinthians 1:3) who "chose us in [Christ] before the foundation of the world ... [and] destined us in love to be his sons" (Ephesians 1:4–5).

A clear expression of God's fatherly care toward Israel as a nation and toward its kings, in particular, is found in a number of places in the Old Testament. But Jews, in their prayers, did not address God directly as their personal Father, even though they did use a formal term for father to respectfully address their superiors, like the king.[52] Most languages also have informal words for "mother" and "father" that are used by children when speaking with their parents. In American English, they are "mom" and "dad."

In Aramaic and Hebrew, the informal, familiar form of address for one's father, used both by young and adult children, is *abba*. But for a Jew to address God as *Abba* in prayer was unheard of in ancient Israel. It would have struck a Jew as irreverent and presumptuous. Not only did Jesus address God this way, however, but he taught his disciples to do the same.

We can further grasp the importance of the word *abba* to the early Christians by the several places where Sts. Mark and Paul, who wrote in Greek, remembered and preserved the word in the original Aramaic form that Christ spoke.[53]

Jesus is the only begotten Son of God. Only he, by nature, can call God *Abba*. We dare to do likewise only because he has shared his sonship with us by his grace. He has allowed us to share his vision and experience of God from the vantage point of beloved sons and daughters. The life of faith, says Pope Francis, is a "filial existence"[54]—that is, the experience of a son or daughter. Walking in faith thus means walking as brothers and sisters in Christ, sons and daughters of the one Father—our Father.

This sort of intimacy and familiarity with God is unprecedented and is unique among the great religions of the world. To this day, the most common address for God in prayer for a Jew is "Lord Our God, King of the Universe." Islam vehemently rejects the very concept of believers being sons and daughters of God or God having any son at all. Buddhism has many things in common with Christianity but not the idea of filial intimacy with a personal God. Viewing God as Father and believing that he invites us to a life of intimate union with him is distinctive of the Christian Faith.

The Father Almighty

So the Father who invites the least of his children to such profound intimacy is at the same time the Almighty, the Sovereign of the vast universe, the builder of galaxies. This is a mind-boggling paradox to say the least.

This is a good time to stop and make an important observation. Divine revelation is full of contrasting, paradoxical truths that are beyond our comprehension, just like this. God is three Persons in one nature. Jesus is fully God and fully man. God is transcendent and so majestic and powerful that it is frightening. Yet, at the same time, he cherishes each person with tenderness, compassion, and mercy.[55]

The tendency of the human mind is to relax the tension and choose one side of a paradox over the other. This is what heresy often does. But, when it comes to the profound mystery of God, to be Catholic is to profess *both/and*, not *either/or*. Committed to the *whole* truth, Catholic Faith respects the mystery of God in all his glorious majesty. Instead of trying to tame the profound mystery of God, faith bows before it. In fact, the Catholic Church defines dogmas to safeguard paradox—to stand as cherubs with swords of fire, protecting the garden of God's mystery, lest it be spoiled by those who would trim it to neat, manageable proportions perfectly comprehensible by the human intellect.[56]

At the name of Jesus
every knee should bow,
in heaven and on earth
and under the earth.

— *Philippians 2:10*

CHAPTER 6

Creation and the Fall

Both the Nicene and Apostles' Creeds identify God, the Father almighty, as the maker or Creator of heaven and earth. In Scripture, the phrase "the heavens and the earth" first appears in the first verse of Genesis. It is Scripture's way of referring to the *totality* of all creation—everything from A to Z.

It is time now to review the marvelous mystery of God's creative work. It is also time to ponder how evil entered God's good world and what implications that has for the story of salvation history.

Creation

Since the rise of modern science, the first eleven chapters of Genesis have been a battleground. If you take the chronology of creation as described in these chapters literalistically (a simplistically literal reading), it would put the time of creation about six thousand years ago. We know now that the universe is about 14 billion years old, give or take a few hundred million years. And, without a doubt, the time from the creation of the first light to Adam and Eve was a lot longer than six days.

Because the Bible is inspired by the Holy Spirit and, therefore, without error, some insist on a literalistic reading of every historical and scientific detail in Genesis, resisting all arguments to the contrary. Others, in the name of science, reject the Bible entirely as a book of unscientific fables.

Interestingly, both sides are making the same mistake. Genesis and the entire Bible were never intended to teach either science or secular history. Their aim is to teach *salvation* history—the unfolding of God's loving plan from its origins to its future consummation. The inspired authors of Scripture teach "truly, faithfully and without error that truth which God desired to put into the sacred writings for our salvation."[57] This is the goal of Genesis and should be what we are looking for when we read Sacred Scripture. The age of the cosmos and the appearance of various life forms are fascinating subjects. But these scientific realities have no bearing on our salvation and are best left to the various scientific disciplines.

The majestic, poetic chapters at the beginning of the Bible do not provide a play-by-play account of *how* things came to be but rather *why* they came to be. Genesis is about the *ultimate* origin, meaning, and purpose of the world and of humanity's unique place in it. These are things science can never tell us.

To greater appreciate just how rich the meaning of the Genesis creation accounts are, it would be helpful to briefly review the creation myth of Israel's next-door neighbors in Mesopotamia. In their account, provided in a poem called the *Enuma Elish*, there were, in the beginning, numerous male and female gods. They, of course, had liaisons and begat divine offspring. These offspring ended up in an intergenerational war of cosmic proportions. The victorious god, Marduk, fashioned the world out of the blood and guts of the defeated dragon goddess of the sea, who happened to be his grandmother.

How different is the biblical teaching! Genesis reveals a God who creates with no need of a consort. He creates in tranquility, dignity, and majesty, like an artist creating a masterpiece of great complexity. It is a process characterized by order, harmony, and goodness. In fact, in the first chapter of Genesis, God takes a step back after each day's work and, admiring what he has done, says, "This is good!"

God is under no compulsion to create. He has no *need*. Unlike us, who make things out of other things, God is the one who "calls into existence the things that do not exist" (Romans 4:17). In other words, he creates out of nothing (*ex nihilo*). The final result is paradise—waters teeming with creatures, the air filled with the songs of innumerable birds, and the earth bearing every kind of tree, laden with fruit.

Creation and the Trinity

The creeds name the Father as the Creator because the Father is the eternal origin of the Son and the Spirit who eternally draw their being from the Father. Hence, the Father is the ultimate source of all reality and so to him we apply the term Creator.

But, to paraphrase the great Church Father Irenaeus, the Father does nothing except by his "two hands," the Son and the Spirit.[58] The work of creation, then, is a trinitarian work in every respect.[59] The Son is the mind of the Father, the divine Word. In Genesis 1, it is through his Word that God creates. God says, "Let there be light," and his Word makes it happen.

Yet it is the Spirit who is identified with the Father's will, which is Love. He is called Spirit because he is the breath of divine life. And, in Genesis 1:1, before God speaks, the Spirit is already hovering over the chaos. The Spirit of God overshadows, the Word of God issues forth, and the void bursts into light and life.

There is amazing intelligence "programmed" into the laws of physics and biology. Where did this *logical* structure come from? It is the imprint of the *Logos*, the Word of God, Jesus Christ, he who is the divine design, reason, and order of all things. He is also the final goal and ultimate purpose of all things, the Omega as well as the Alpha. St. Paul, in his letter to the Colossians says, "All things were created through him and for him. He is before all things, and in him all things hold together" (Colossians 1:16–17).

Why did God create a logical universe that is "held together" through his Logos? Pope Francis answers: "God's love is the fundamental moving force in all created things." Dante writes of "the love which moves the sun and stars."[60] This power of love is a Person—God's Holy Spirit. At times, people talk of the "life-force" present in the universe. This force is the same Person, the Lord and Giver of Life himself. We see an amazing web of relationships in nature, which form a vast ecosystem. Everything in it is marvelously interconnected and interdependent. Where does this amazing bond of life come from, which keeps all created things working as one harmonious whole? This bond was brought into being by the eternal bond of love between the Father and the Son: the Spirit of love, unity, and harmony.

God as Intimately Involved

Often, when people think about God as the first cause of the universe, they imagine God getting the ball rolling and then letting nature take its course. The Deists of the seventeenth- and eighteenth-century Enlightenment, who influenced Thomas Jefferson and many of the American Founding Fathers, thought this way.[61] They depicted God as a clockmaker who designed the world like an intricate Swiss timepiece. He created it, wound it up, and retired from the scene, letting the clock run on its own according to its own mechanism.

This is not at all the Christian doctrine of creation. God is transcendent and distinct from creation, but he is very much present, or *immanent*, within it. His presence never ceases sustaining, developing, and guiding it to its ultimate perfection. The three divine Persons are actively sustaining the existence of all things and drawing everything toward its ultimate purpose in the fullness of time, which is for all things to be united in Christ (see Ephesians 1:10) and transformed into what the book of Revelation calls "a new heaven and a new earth" (Revelation 21:1).

God is so intensely involved in the working of nature that, should the Trinity ever withdraw themselves from the scene for even a split second, we would not just die; rather, we and the world would simply disappear—lapsing back into the nothingness of which we were created.

The amazing thing is that each of the many creatures fashioned by the Trinity has its own distinct nature. God's continued presence and ceaseless activity do not compete with his creatures' own natural activity. Rather, God works through these creatures and the various laws of nature, which all have their origin in his Word. This is the mystery of Divine Providence.

So creation is not just the initial moment. It is an ongoing process over which the Trinity actively presides. The Holy Spirit, said Pope St. John

Paul II, possesses infinite creativity. He fills the world with possibilities, with potential that is yet to be actualized. Creation is a work of art. And God is still painting.[62]

Creation as a Book

A common theme in the writings of the Church Fathers is that there are three books about God—the book of creation, the book of the human soul, and the book of the Sacred Scriptures. The revelation conveyed in the last of these three gives us eyes to see God's presence in the first two.

Psalm 19 opens with this line: "The heavens are telling the glory of God; and the firmament proclaims his handiwork." Creation itself cannot help but manifest the beauty of its Creator, who is himself infinite beauty. The world, fashioned by the divine artist, is a sort of revelation since everywhere it contains reflections of his glory. Each creature has a purpose; each manifests some aspect of God's goodness.

In the book of Revelation, the four living creatures symbolize all creatures, great and small, from the four corners of the world, worshipping God before the throne. Creation was created to glorify its maker and so share in his glory. The birds singing in the morning are inviting us to join them in their hymn of praise.

Though many speak of "Mother Nature," the word *nature* comes from the word for "that which is born." It is more appropriate, from the biblical point of view, to call the earth our sister, as did St. Francis of Assisi. His *Canticle of the Creatures* and Pope Francis's encyclical *Laudato Si'* beckon us to cultivate a sense of praise and wonder for Brother Sun, Sister Moon, and the entire garden of creation. Our response should be to join in creation's symphony of praise with the help of the psalms, which more than any other Bible texts, help us to glorify the Lord for and with his creatures.

Human Uniqueness

Two accounts of creation are found in the Bible in the first two chapters of Genesis. Both emphasize man and woman as the pinnacle of the created world. In Genesis 1, after each day of creation, God admires his work and judges it to be good. After the sixth day, on which he creates man and woman, he proclaims it to be *very* good (see Genesis 1:31).

Only human beings are created in the image and likeness of God (see Genesis 1:26). We are like the Trinity in two important ways. First, the triune God is rational and free. He has an intellect and will. So we, too, have been given intellect and will, which means that we are not driven by brute instinct but have the ability to give ourselves freely in love.

Second, we are created for loving relationship after the pattern of the triune God. God did not just make man individually in his own image and likeness; rather, he made man *and* woman in his image and likeness. And the love between a man and woman is itself creative, resulting in the generation of children. The eternal loving communion of Father, Son, and Holy Spirit is beautifully reflected in the loving union of a husband and wife and their children.[63]

Thus, the very purpose of creation is ultimately to create a space for *covenant*—a setting for humanity to encounter God and enter into communion with him.[64] Since we are the only creatures willed by God for our own sake, human dignity is inviolable.[65]

While human beings are given *dominion* over creation (see Genesis 1:26, 28), we are nonetheless *responsible* for creation, precisely because we are unique.[66] We are stewards—not owners—of the gift of creation. We are unique in that we can become aware of God's providential ordering of creation and can *choose* to participate in it, both for ourselves and for the rest of creation.[67]

Angels and Demons

The reference in Genesis 1:1 to God creating the heavens and earth includes the angelic world. The Nicene Creed makes this inclusion explicit by stating that God is the creator of heaven and earth, of "all things visible and invisible"—namely, spirits.

Angels are creatures. They are not eternal like God, but they are created out of nothing. They are non-corporeal (that is, without bodies) spiritual creatures (see CCC 330). And they are by nature superior to us, especially in terms of the power of their intellect.

The Bible reveals the presence of some of these spirits as angels or messengers. Some, like Raphael, Gabriel, and Michael (see Tobit 12:15-22; Daniel 9:20-27; Luke 1:26–28; Revelation 12:7-12), play an important role in salvation history and are called archangels. Some serve as protectors, including the Archangel Michael and the guardian angels (see Matthew 18:10). The Old Testament refers to other classes of these creatures as seraphim (literally "burning ones") and cherubim (see Isaiah 6:2–3 and Ezekiel 10:14). St. Paul refers to still other classes of them as thrones, dominions, principalities, and powers (see Colossians 1:16; Ephesians 6:12). Thus, in the invisible realm, there appears to be the same manifold diversity that we see in the visible world.

Angels, like men, are rational and free. And God desires from rational creatures the free response of love. The gift of intellect and will, given to angels as well as human beings, makes this possible. But freedom also makes possible a choice against love. The Church teaches that all angels, at the beginning of their existence, had to make an irrevocable choice for or against God. We often make wrong choices based on ignorance; we often fail to see all the destructive consequences of wrong choices and so, later, change our minds. The angelic intellect sees and knows the consequences of choices to a far greater degree, and so, once the angelic choice is made, it is firm and irrevocable. This means that once their decision is made, angels are destined for eternal communion with God in heaven or eternal separation from God in hell. There is no failure on the part of God's mercy here; rather, the angelic creatures that chose to reject God have permanently hardened their hearts, so to speak, against him (see CCC 392–393).

Like the good angels, fallen angels or demons are also active in our lives. But they loathe us, resenting the fact that the eternal Son joined himself to human flesh (see John 8:44). Out of envy (see Wisdom 2:24), they seek to prevent us from sharing his glory. Therefore, the demonic world has human sin and destruction as its chief mission.

We should be careful not to be too enamored with the sensational here. C.S. Lewis, in his *Screwtape Letters*,[68] is exactly right when he points out that the Devil would love for us to disbelieve in his existence; we would then become easy targets. But Satan would equally like us to become overly fascinated by him and, thereby, dabble in witchcraft and the occult. This sort of unhealthy curiosity also leads to spiritual ruin.

We remember what St. Paul taught us: "At the *name of Jesus* every knee should bow, in heaven and on earth and *under the earth*" (Philippians 2:10; emphasis added). This means that the demons tremble at the power of the Holy Name of Jesus. Therefore, we need not fear. Satan is like a fierce dog on a chain. His bark is frightening, but we have nothing to fear if we remain united to Christ. As Jesus has said, "In the world you have tribulation; but be of good cheer, I have overcome the world" (John 16:33).

At the same time, we must be vigilant to avoid the traps of the Devil through sin or occult practices. "Submit yourselves therefore to God. Resist the devil and he will flee from you" (James 4:7).

The Fall

If Genesis 1 reveals the majesty of God as Creator of all things, Genesis 2 zooms in on the mystery of God's intimate relation with mankind in the Garden of Eden. This setting in paradise is a symbolic way to show primordial humanity in a state of friendship and communion with God (see CCC 374–376).

The Lord gives Adam a test, but, first, he is emphatic about Adam's freedom as a child of God: "You may *freely eat of every tree* of the garden; but of the tree of the knowledge of good and evil you shall not eat, for in the day that you eat of it you shall die" (Genesis 2:16–17; emphasis added).

When the serpent approaches the woman in the garden, he seeks to plant doubt in her heart about the nature of God's decree and paints it as tyrannical, suggesting that God is holding something back from Adam and Eve— something they could attain if only they would eat the forbidden fruit: "You will not die," the serpent says, "for God knows that when you eat of it *your eyes will be opened,* and *you will be like God,* knowing good and evil" (Genesis 3:4–5; emphasis added).

This is not simply a temptation to *recognize* what is good and evil. Rather, the temptation is to be the one who *decides* what is good and evil—that is, to take the place of God (see CCC 396). The decision to follow the serpent's suggestion and disobey God is a twofold sin. It is a sin against faith, for it doubts God's goodness and love and, therefore, doubts the truthfulness of his Word. It is also a sin of pride, a refusal to accept the stature of the creature and, instead, to reach out and grasp for divine status.

The consequences of Adam and Eve's choice are disastrous. They undergo, first, a spiritual death, which ruptures a series of harmonies: with God, with each other, within themselves, and even with creation. This leads to physical death as well (see Genesis 3:19; CCC 400).

The forfeiture of this graced state in the garden results in what is known as "concupiscence," an inclination towards sin—behavior that is both self-destructive and injurious to our neighbor. This is what explains the experience that St. Paul describes so well: Sometimes we know what we should do, and still we do not do it, and often we desire to do what we know we should not do (see Romans 7:15). St. Paul calls this disordered tendency the "law of sin" (Romans 7:23) or "the flesh" (Galatians 5:19–24).

"Original sin," then, refers both to the first sin of Adam and Eve and to the fallen nature we now inherit from them. Adam and Eve pass on to us a nature that is good but deeply wounded. Our intellects are now darkened, our wills weakened, and our passions in disarray (see CCC 404–405).

God is a loving Father. Satan is a ruthless tyrant. Sin makes us slaves of the Evil One, who "through fear of death" makes us "subject to lifelong bondage" (Hebrews 2:15; see CCC 407). Baptism restores us to a life of grace and delivers us from Satan's tyranny. Yet a degree of concupiscence remains in the baptized, though we are no longer controlled by it. By the power of the Spirit, we can and must resist our sinful inclinations, crucifying the flesh "with its passions and desires" (Galatians 5:24). In God's providence, there is merit in our struggle; by allowing some consequences of original sin to remain—concupiscence, suffering, and death—the Lord seeks to facilitate our transformation, strengthen us in virtue, and conform us to Christ Jesus (see Romans 8:29 and CCC 409).

How Literally Should I Take Adam and Eve?

The account of the fall of Adam and Eve is clearly told in a way that is deeply symbolic and poetic. There are two extremes to avoid here (and in general this applies to all of Genesis 1–11). On the one hand, we want to avoid reading the Adam and Eve story as straightforward history. On the other hand, we also want to avoid the view that sees these early chapters of Genesis as nothing but myth—that is, as *only* symbolic, with no reality behind them.

Rather, the story of Adam and Eve relates something that really happened at the dawn of human history, but which is recounted in a deeply symbolic and figurative way. The *Catechism* is especially clear on this point: "The account of the fall in *Genesis* 3 uses figurative language, but affirms a primeval event, a deed that took place *at the beginning of the history of man.*[69] Revelation gives us the certainty of faith that the whole of human history is marked by the original fault freely committed by our first parents"[70] (CCC 390). The *Catechism* continues, "We cannot tamper with the revelation of original sin without undermining the mystery of Christ" (CCC 389).

We might say, then, that these early chapters of Genesis narrate real *history* but in a *symbolic* way.

The Goodness of Creation

Creation shares in God's goodness. This is very important because early heresies opposed it, denigrating the body and viewing material creation as evil. That train of thought tends to recur throughout history.[71] It sees the human person in a dualistic way—as if the human being were fundamentally two separate entities: a *body* and an *interior reality* imprisoned within the body. Dualism puts the body and the material world in opposition to the soul and the spiritual world. In contrast, Scripture and Catholic Tradition teach that while human beings do possess a material body and spiritual soul, our souls are not imprisoned in our bodies. We are a body-soul composite, fundamentally one thing, one being.[72]

But there are strong movements today to see our physical bodies as distinct from and perhaps even opposed to who we really are—suggesting that our true selves are somehow nothing more than a form of consciousness trapped in our bodies. Thus, instead of recognizing the God-givenness of our bodies, some would wish to manipulate the body to make it conform to one's self-understanding. Those struggling with various manifestations of this confusion, such as gender dysphoria, need always to be treated with the utmost compassion. But we should be alert to the erroneous principles undergirding activists within this movement—especially the dualistic thinking that sees the body as not essential to who we are.[73]

To affirm God as Creator is to affirm the *givenness* of creation—whether in nature or in our own bodies. We are not the masters of creation; we are not its owners who can do with it as we please in opposition to God's designs and plans for our lives. As Pope Francis insists in his encyclical *Laudato Si'*, the damage done to the natural and social environment is "due to the same evil: the notion that there are no indisputable truths to guide our lives ... [that] human freedom is limitless."[74]

If there is a *givenness* to creation—an objective order of things—then our freedom is not absolute. Instead, we are meant to use our freedom to work with the divinely inscribed order written into creation and not seek to endlessly manipulate it to our own ends. Pope Francis connects the exploitation of the environment *with the unwillingness to accept our bodies as God-given*, seeing them as two instances of the same human dysfunction—namely, a thirst for absolute power and unbridled freedom:

> The acceptance of our bodies as God's gift is vital for welcoming and accepting the entire world as a gift from the Father and our common home, *whereas thinking we enjoy absolute power over our bodies turns, often subtly, into thinking we enjoy absolute power over creation*. Learning to accept our body, to care for it and to respect its fullest meaning, is an essential element of any genuine human ecology.[75]

Promise of Redemption

What is interesting in the narrative of the Fall is what Satan appears to get right. The Devil assured Adam and Eve that they would not die, and they did not die immediately—at least, not *physically*. The Devil assured them that upon eating the fruit their eyes would be opened—and their eyes were opened, but, ironically, what they saw was a newfound shame (see Genesis 3:7). Humanity's posture toward God now became one of fear: "I heard the sound of you in the garden, and I was afraid" (Genesis 3:10).

Yet God does not give up on his good creation. Indeed, in Genesis 3:15, we have the first promise of redemption: "I will put enmity between you [the Evil One] and the woman, and between your seed and her seed; he shall bruise your head, and you shall bruise his heel."

This prophecy is cryptic, but it points to the ultimate defeat of the Evil One by the woman's messianic offspring, who is wounded in the process ("you shall bruise his heel"). In John's Gospel, when the apostle refers to Mary consistently as "woman," he is portraying her as the fulfillment of this prophecy—the "woman" who bears the seed (Jesus) who defeats Satan once and for all.[76]

This prophecy in Genesis is known as the *protoevangelium* (Latin for "first Gospel") because it is the first promise of redemption after the Fall. The rest of salvation history prepares the way for its momentous fulfillment in the fullness of time.

God does not abandon his people. He keeps his promises to the very end; he even enters his own story to do it, as we will see in the next chapter.

CHAPTER 7

Jesus, God with Us

If the creed is the heart of the Catholic Faith, then the second stanza, which focuses on Jesus, is the heart of the creed. It stands in the very middle of it because Jesus Christ is the center not only of our faith but of absolutely everything in heaven and on earth. Everything in nature and history comes together in his Person and his saving work.[77]

Before we discuss his identity and his incarnation in this chapter, and the climax of his saving work in the next, we need to briefly review what happened between the promise made in the Garden and the arrival of Christ in a stable in Bethlehem.

Prepare the Way

The great theme of the preaching of Jesus' cousin, St. John the Baptist, was a text from Isaiah 40:3: "Prepare the way of the LORD." This sums up the entire story of salvation history from Adam to John. It was all one vast preparation for Jesus, the Promised One.

Things quickly deteriorated after the fall of Adam and Eve. Sin became like a snowball rolling down a snowy hill; it just got larger and more dangerous with every passing moment. Wickedness swamped the world, so God decided to wash it away with a flood of epic, indeed biblical, proportions. Noah and seven from his family were saved in the Ark, along with the animals necessary to repopulate the earth. But, while the waters scrubbed the surface of the earth, they failed to cleanse the hearts of Noah and his family. Even these "decent" folk had the hidden wound of original sin and so repopulated the world with the same broken humanity as before (see Genesis 7–10).

This led to the arrogance of Babel and its tower (see Genesis 11). With Babel, civilization had arrived, but it was anything but civilized. It only served to institutionalize sin as a structural, cultural reality. Societies opposed to God have been with us ever since, working together with "the flesh" (concupiscence) and the Devil to make it very difficult for anyone to act virtuously. Scripture sometimes refers to this culture of sin and death as "the world." When used in this sense, "world" does not refer to God's beautiful creation or to the world's people whom God loves (see John 3:16). Here "the world" means society gone bad and in league with the Evil One (see 1 John 5:19).

God's rescue mission began with Abraham (see Genesis 12) and continued with his son Isaac, and his son Jacob. God made a series of promises to Abraham, Isaac, and Jacob, which included the promise of numerous descendants and a homeland where they would dwell securely. There was even a mysterious promise that somehow by Abraham "all the families of the earth shall bless themselves" (Genesis 12:3) and kings would come forth from him (see Genesis 17:4–8).

Abraham's great-grandsons became the patriarchs of twelve tribes. They migrated into Egypt to escape famine but were ultimately enslaved. So God raised up Moses to bring them out of Egypt in a great act of liberation. But Pharoah, understandably, was reluctant to let his free labor walk away. He needed to be persuaded by a series of plagues. The last and greatest chastisement sent by God was the angel of death to claim the first-born of man and beast (see Exodus 11–12). Only the mysterious blood of a sacrificed lamb, swabbed on the doorposts and lintels of their houses, would save the Israelites from the angel of death.

After this blow, Pharoah could not get rid of the Israelites fast enough. So they set out for a rendezvous with God in the desert, except that a sea stood in their way. Pharoah, who then changed his mind again about letting them go, pursued them with horses and chariots. He thought he had them trapped, pinned between his forces and the sea. But God opened the sea and brought the Israelites safely through the midst of it, letting the waters flow back upon the onrushing enemy and destroying them (see Exodus 14).

In this mysterious sequence of Passover and Exodus, God revealed himself as the Israelites' redeemer, their savior from both slavery and death. He had saved them, however, for a purpose: to enter into a covenant with himself so that they would become his most precious possession, his own royal and priestly people (see Exodus 19:4–6). So he gave them a distinctive way of life, expressed in the Ten Commandments (see Exodus 20), along with many other instructions, known together as the Law, or Torah. And he gave them a priesthood to offer sacrifice for them and lead them in holiness and divine worship.

Yet, within days of receiving the Law, they violated the very first commandment: to worship no other gods besides God. And, ironically, the one who led them in this treason was Aaron, the chief priest appointed by Moses to lead the worship of the one God. The problem seemed to be that the Law of God had been inscribed on tablets of stone but not on the hearts of the people (see Exodus 32).

God next intended to lead them to the land he had promised to their forefathers. They marched behind the Ark of the Covenant (see Exodus 25:10; Numbers 10:35), the bearer of the stone tablets and of God's presence, with the luminous cloud of God's glory to lead them by day and a pillar of fire by night (see Exodus 13:21–22; 40:34-38). But, because of their constant grumbling and disobedience, a journey that should have taken forty days took forty years. Even Moses faltered in a critical moment at Meribah, failing to believe God, and failing to model for the people perfect obedience and divine patience (see Numbers 20:11–13). As a result, he and Aaron were not allowed to enter the Promised Land.

Once in the land, the people kept being drawn to the pagan practices of its inhabitants. God had to allow their enemies to harass them, for this seemed the only thing that would wake them up. They cried out for deliverance, so God gave them judges and kings to deliver and protect them. Yet even the best of these shepherds, David, preyed on the sheep he was supposed to protect; he stole the wife of one of his most loyal officers and had the man killed to cover up the crime (see 2 Samuel 11–12; Psalm 51).

To his credit, his son Solomon constructed the Temple in Jerusalem—the visible sign that the one God dwelt among his people. Yet to his shame Solomon, too, became an idolator, seduced by his riches and his many foreign wives. His son was worse, provoking the people to civil war. Tragically, the alienating power of sin split the twelve tribes into two warring peoples— Israel in the north and Judah in the south (see 1 Kings 11–12).

The kings and priests of both kingdoms were so bad that God had to raise up spokesmen called prophets, filled with the Spirit, to call his people to repentance. In general, the people and their leaders paid little heed to these messengers. And so God's people brought disaster upon themselves: the two most important things to them, the land and the Temple, were taken from them, and they were dragged into exile. Only a tiny remnant from the two southern tribes eventually returned, but not as a free, independent people—and no longer with their own anointed king. David's dynasty was no more. The Temple and the city lay in ruins.

The people had broken the covenant made at Sinai. Priests, prophets, and kings had not been enough. The gifts of the Temple and the land had not been enough. So God now spoke through his prophets to promise what would be enough: At some future time, God would make with them a *new* covenant (see Jeremiah 31:31–34). He would give them a *new* heart, a heart of flesh, and inscribe his Law upon it (see Ezekiel 36:25–29). He would pour out his Spirit so that everyone, not just a select few, would be his prophets (see Joel 2:28–29). And he would send them an anointed Messiah, a Savior. Various messianic figures were described in different oracles: a prophet like Moses (see Deuteronomy 18:18), a king like David (see Isaiah 11:1), a suffering servant (see Isaiah 52–53), a glorious "son of man" (Daniel 7:13–14). The future anointed one, whoever he might be, would usher in a new age when things would be different, when wine would drip from the mountaintops (see Isaiah 25:6; Joel 3:18; Amos 9:13–14) and a fountain would spring from the house of the Lord (see Ezekiel 47; Joel 3:18; Zechariah 13:1; 14:8).

Priests, prophets, and kings had all been anointed by God. The Jewish people were not sure which of these the coming figure would be, but they were expecting a sort of super-anointed one, a messiah greater than any priest, prophet, or king they had seen before.

The Word Made Flesh

Yet no one seemed to expect a messiah who would be all three wrapped up in one—a prophetic, priestly, kingly messiah. And, in their wildest dreams, they never conceived of God coming to assume this role himself, in the flesh. But that is exactly what he did. "The Word became flesh and dwelt among us" (John 1:14). Who would ever imagine that the Eternal Word, who made the universe, could become an infant—a babe incapable of speech? Or that the Most High would stoop so low as to be born amid the squalor of a stable? Inconceivable.[78]

Fully God

There are many ways that Jesus shows himself in the Gospels to be more than a prophet, more than a teacher, more than simply a great man. His divinity is one of the chief messages of John's Gospel in particular (see John 1:1; 20:28).

But the teaching is everywhere in the New Testament and early Catholic Tradition—in Paul's letters, in Hebrews, and in the book of Revelation, to name a few. St. Paul says that in Christ "the whole fulness of deity dwells bodily" (Colossians 2:9). In seven brief letters written on his way to martyrdom just a few years after the last New Testament book was written, St. Ignatius, bishop of Antioch, explicitly calls Jesus "God" no less than sixteen times.

So, when the Arian heresy arose in the fourth century and claimed that the Word made flesh was not eternal but was, rather, the first and greatest of God's creatures, it was a novelty. Arius regarded Jesus not as fully God but only partly God, as a sort of demi-god or half-god. The bishops at the first council of Nicaea (AD 325), who convened to respond to this threat, were doing no more than defending Scripture and Tradition.[79]

The council expanded a typical baptismal creed to make it unambiguously clear that Jesus is fully God. He is "God from God, light from light, true God from true God." His nature is not simply *like* God; he is fully divine, consubstantial (of one substance) with the Father. This means the Son has the very same divine nature as the Father, which includes eternity, without beginning or end. This is actually what the last line of the "Glory be" teaches us: "As it was in the beginning, is now, and ever shall be" means that the Father, Son, and Spirit are coeternal. They always were, they are, and they are to come, and to each of the three is due equally the fullness of divine worship and glory.

The *Only* Son of God

When we speak of the Son as only begotten (see John 1:14), we have to realize that the analogy of human begetting is not exact. A human father pre-exists his son. He begets him in a moment in time, and, before that moment, the son did not exist. In the case of the Son, the Word, there was never a time when he was not. "Begotten not made" means he was not begotten in a moment in time: His Father gives him being eternally; he is *eternally* begotten of the Father.

Both the Apostles' Creed and the Nicene Creed underline the fact that Jesus is the only Son of God.

In the Old Testament, angels are sometimes called "sons of God" (see Genesis 6:2, 4; Job 1:6). The entire people of Israel were referred to as the Lord's son (see Exodus 4:22). And so was the reigning king (see Psalm 89:26–27). All human beings, in a sense, are children of God, and all Christians are his sons and daughters in an even deeper way. Yet none of these uses of the term implies that anyone—the angels, the nation, the king, Christians, or humanity in general—is in any way equal in nature to God the Father. Christians are children of God in an adopted sense because of God's gracious choice to share his divine life with us and welcome us, his creatures, into communion with him. But Jesus is the natural, not adopted, Son of God. He is God's Son in an absolutely unique way. In the *Gloria*, an ancient prayer of the Western Church, we confess this. Speaking to Jesus we cry,

"You *alone* are the Holy One, you *alone* are the Lord, you *alone* are the Most High!" (*Roman Missal*, Order of Mass; emphasis added).

Fullness of Truth

One implication of this is that Jesus and only Jesus is the fullness of truth, the final Word of God, since he is the Word made flesh. The Law and all the prophets who came before him brought provisional and incomplete revelations about God. The letter to the Hebrews puts it well: "In times past, God spoke in partial and various ways to our ancestors through the prophets; in these last days, he spoke to us through a son, whom he made heir of all things and through whom he created the universe" (Hebrews 1:1–2; NABRE).[80]

In Jesus, God has said everything there is to say. Apostles, prophets, apparitions, and visions that come after him bring no new revelation; they just help us unpack the unfathomable riches already contained in the Person and work of Jesus Christ (see Ephesians 3:8).

Other Religions?

The history of salvation is particularly the story of the people of Israel up until the Incarnation. Jesus broadens the people of God to include people of every tribe and tongue, people and nation. What about those peoples and nations before the coming of Jesus? They produced people still revered today as teachers of wisdom, from Plato and Aristotle to Confucius and Buddha. Is there anything of value in the thought of such people?

If Jesus is the Eternal Word through whom all things were made, then his imprint is reflected in human reason, even though that reason is darkened by original sin. So St. Justin Martyr, a second-century Father of the Church, discerns "seeds of the Word" scattered throughout the ideas of many human teachers over the course of time. This is not full-blown divine wisdom but rather fragmentary truth in seed-form, some kernels of wheat that need to be purified of chaff, ground, and joined with other kernels to be made into the bread of life-giving truth. This is done only through the Son, the Eternal Word and the Bread of Life himself, who is the fullness of Truth. He is the norm and sieve by which the chaff of ignorance and sin is removed, the Bread of Truth into which all other kernels, ground, must be kneaded to provide the complete nourishment that people crave.

The Catholic Church honors truth wherever it may be found because all truth comes from the Divine Word. And only in him does the fragmentary truth of the Law and the prophets, the Gentile philosophers and seers, find its completion and Catholic fullness.

Fully Man

In the Old Testament, it is only God who is the Savior and Redeemer of the people.[81] He uses various prophets, kings, and priests as his anointed instruments, but only God saves and redeems. If Jesus were not truly God, he could not be our Savior. If he were not truly God, then God sent us merely his prime minister—another anointed instrument and mediator, still keeping us at arm's length from himself.

The promise of a king who is Emmanuel, truly God-with-us, is fulfilled in Jesus (see Isaiah 7:14). The Temple was the dwelling place of God's Name,[82] the place on earth where the people could be as close to God as possible. In the Temple, Israel could come close to God. But, in Jesus, God becomes wholly present to us, not just God's Name but God himself in our midst. The humanity of Jesus is the new Temple, the new and true meeting place of heaven and earth.[83]

For all these reasons, heresies denying the divinity of Christ were vigorously resisted in the early Church. But other heresies denying the fullness of humanity were strongly rebuffed as well. There was a succession of these. The earliest one denied that God, as pure spirit, would ever dirty his hands with the muck and mire of this material world. So, it reasoned, Jesus must have only *appeared* to be a human being, much like the three angels who visited Abraham on their way to Sodom (see Genesis 18). Jesus' birth and death, for these heretics, were merely an illusion because his body was only an apparition.

Another heretical theory was that the Word truly appropriated a human body in Jesus of Nazareth but took the place of its human soul. So Jesus was just God driving a human body around like a car. He had no human mind or human will. Still others said Jesus was a confused blend of God and man, so that he did not have a human nature like ours; he was more like a kind of superman. Though he looked like us, as Clark Kent looked like a human being, he had no real human limitations, like needing to sleep, eat, or learn.

The Fathers of the Church battled these heresies as vigorously as they fought the denials of Jesus' divinity. They knew that if Jesus were not fully God, he could not be our Savior. But they were also convinced that if he were not fully man, we would not be saved either. We will discuss the saving work of Christ further in our next chapter. But here we must point this out: What we needed to be saved from most of all was our separation from God and our wounded human nature, which could only be healed by the restoration of communion with him.

The Incarnation was actually the beginning of Redemption, the reconciliation of heaven and earth. In the moment of the Incarnation in Mary's womb, the divine Word was perfectly united with an entire human nature. He became like us in all things but sin.[84]

Another name for redemption or salvation is atonement, or at-one-ment. It is the restoration of unity between God and man, bringing them together again as one. This process of reconciliation and reunion began when the Word became flesh in Mary's womb. In this place and in this moment, when the divine Word was inseparably united with a complete human nature, the healing of our wounded nature began as well.

If you think about it, the real source of our sin is our soul. We only sin with our body because of our wounded mind and will. If the divine Word had taken a human body only, then our souls would have been left out of the atonement and would be still alienated from him. A perfect, full humanity in perfect communion with God is what was required. This communion, first achieved in the man Jesus, would later be extended to the members of his Body, which is what our next chapter is about.

The Image of the Unseen God

We are accustomed to the word *icon* meaning either a symbol on our computer screen or a religious painting venerated in Eastern Christianity. We may not be aware that *ikon* is simply the Greek word for "image."

This is significant because, in the Ten Commandments, God stipulates that his people are not to make for themselves "graven images" of animal or human forms that they would then worship since this was the form of idolatry practiced by the peoples surrounding the Israelites (see Exodus 20:4–5). Yet, in giving us Jesus, God himself provided us with "the image [icon] of the invisible God" (Colossians 1:15).

From the earliest centuries, Christians, therefore, depicted Christ, "the icon of God," in art.[85] They also depicted the human images of members of his Body, the saints, through whom his light radiates.

This practice was widespread and without controversy until armies of Muslim Arabs won some battles over Byzantine armies that marched behind Christian icons. The victorious Muslims were known to vehemently reject all images as idolatrous. A Byzantine general who later became emperor apparently surmised that these defeats were God's judgment on Christians for not obeying, as the Muslims did, the prohibition of images in Exodus. He, therefore, began a program of *iconoclasm*, or destruction of images.

An ecumenical council was called to deal with the crisis. It judged that to deny the legitimacy of icons was to deny the humanity of Christ; if Jesus were indeed true God and true man, then divinity had become visible in his humanity, and this humanity could be depicted in art. Such icons can and should be honored as an aid to our devotion but not worshipped. Images of the saints, members of his body and true extensions of his humanity, can and should be honored as well. Veneration of all such objects passes from the artistic images to the Image himself, from the icons to the Icon.

So the use of images in devotion is nothing more than a corollary to Catholic belief in the Incarnation, in God truly becoming man.

The God-Bearer

Devotion to Mary, the mother of Jesus, is also something that was widespread in the earliest centuries of the Church. It was traditional by the fourth and fifth centuries, when the battles raged over Jesus' full humanity and divinity. One prominent churchman, the patriarch Nestorius, caused a ruckus when he publicly proclaimed that Mary should not be called by the traditional title "God-bearer" or "Mother of God." God, he explained, could not have a mother. Mary should instead be called "Mother of Christ."

Squeamishness about calling Mary "God-bearer" or "Mother of God" really boiled down to a denial of the unity of Christ's Person as inseparably both God and man from the moment of his conception. The ecumenical Council of Ephesus, recognizing this, condemned Nestorius and officially defined what the people for centuries had already expressed in their devotion: that Mary is truly the *Theotokos*, the God-bearer, or Mother of God. From that moment, churches began to be dedicated to her honor, and devotion to her increased.

Ark of the Covenant

In the Old Testament, if anything could be called the "God-bearer," it was the Ark of the Covenant, the seat of God's glorious cloud of presence. This God-bearer contained the tablets of the Ten Commandments, the Word of God inscribed by the finger of God.

The Gospel of Luke shows us that Mary is the Ark of the New Covenant. She is overshadowed by the Spirit (see Luke 1:35) as the Ark was overshadowed by the cloud of glory. She contained within herself not simply the written words of God but the Eternal Word of God himself, who had taken flesh drawn from her body. Newly pregnant, she carried the Word within her to the hill country of Judea, where John the Baptist leapt before him just as David had danced before the Ark.[86]

Honor paid to Mary, God-bearer and Ark of the New Covenant, proceeds directly from recognizing who Jesus really is: fully God and fully man, made flesh in her womb. If the Ark of the Old Covenant was treated with extraordinary reverence, how more appropriate to honor the Ark of the New Covenant.

Mary is mentioned by name in the second stanza of the creed for this reason. Proper devotion to Christ, the Incarnate Word, also appreciates the role that Mary, the Mother of God, played in God's gift of his Son for our salvation.

CHAPTER 8

Jesus Christ, Redeemer

There is no symbol more distinctively Christian than the Cross. Virtually everyone in western society is so familiar with it that they are, for the most part, desensitized to it. For people in Jesus' day, the cross was not a religious symbol. Rather, it was a horror and a curse. It was the most shameful and painful way to die, a punishment reserved by Rome for slaves and conquered peoples.

Yet this symbol of terror and disgrace stands dead center in the central stanza of the creed and at the center of Catholic faith.

Why is this? And why did torture and death have to be the necessary price of salvation? Couldn't God just have wiped the slate clean and acquitted the human race by judicial fiat?

This is the mystery we will probe in this chapter. But here we must call to mind something noted very early on in this book. We are dealing here with something that does not neatly fit into human categories. The biblical authors speak of Jesus' work in terms of analogies drawn from human life and foreshadowings in the history of salvation. No one image or analogy is adequate to fully explain his saving work. Yet we have chosen to focus on a Pauline image emphasized by many of the Fathers of the Church, which can help us gain new insight and answer many of our questions.

Recapitulation: A New Head, a New Start

From the start, we were intended by God to be a family and a nation. Every family has a head, as does every nation. The responsibility of the head is to lead. In the case of the family and nation of God, the head had the role to lead in the way of trust, obedience, and love of God. The two great commandments that summed up the whole Law are these: to love God with one's whole heart and to love one's neighbor as oneself.

The first head of the human race, Adam, failed in this task, leading his descendants down a path of self-destruction and estrangement from God. As God began a new family, that of Abraham, Isaac, and Jacob, leaders called "messiahs"—anointed ones of God—failed again and again to love wholeheartedly. Aaron, the first high priest, failed. Moses, the greatest of the prophets, failed. David and all the kings after him failed.

What both Israel and the entire human race needed was a new head who would not fail. This new head would give Israel a new start by being the first to live out these two great commandments totally and completely, throughout the whole span of his life. The righteousness of this head would not only have to be sufficient to lead others into righteousness; it would have to be of such a magnitude as to offset and blot out all human unrighteousness from the beginning of time. The righteousness won and communicated by this head to those who came after would have to be more than a divine acquittal; it had to be a real righteousness that could penetrate to the core of the person, melting hearts of stone and transforming them into hearts of flesh.

Someone had to be a new Adam, living all the stages of human life and, by living in perfect communion with the Father, undoing centuries of mankind's estrangement from God. That someone had to be the perfect prophet, God's perfect spokesperson, speaking the fullness of God's Word without disobeying like Jonah or complaining like Jeremiah. Someone had to be the perfect king, who never ceased to protect and feed the sheep, who never preyed upon them as David had done. Someone needed to be the perfect priest, who offered the perfect, unsurpassable sacrifice that would suffice until the end of time. Such a one would *recapitulate*—relive and redo—not only the history of Israel but the entire story of the human race.

This is what was needed. And Jesus was fully equipped for this purpose. The Word became flesh as if to say to the Father, "Behold, I have come to do your will" (Hebrews 10:9). His whole purpose for coming down from heaven was, as the Nicene Creed declares, "for us men and for our salvation."

His birth, as we have seen, was the beginning of the saving work of atonement. The "hidden years" before the launch of his ministry also play a role. All that we know of his childhood is all we need to know: He had a hunger for God, and he was obedient to his parents. He wholeheartedly embraced the task of youth to grow in wisdom, age, and grace. Thus, he recapitulated and sanctified childhood. He did the same as a young man who, like his foster-father Joseph,[87] worked with his hands, sanctifying work, which is such an important part of human life.

His Baptism, Anointing, and Ministry

Jesus was conceived by the Holy Spirit and was filled with that Spirit throughout his life. But, at his baptism, there came a new outpouring that signaled an important change. Before he began his public ministry, Jesus descended into the waters of the Jordan and was baptized by his cousin John. He did this not because he needed forgiveness but because, as the new head, he needed to lead Israel and all humanity on the road of repentance—the road back to God. As he emerged from the water, the Spirit of God descended upon him in visible form and the Father's voice was heard identifying him as his beloved Son.

The anointing of priests, prophets, and kings was done with a perfumed oil that symbolized the Holy Spirit. Here, the Holy Spirit himself anoints Jesus' sacred humanity publicly, manifesting him as the Messiah, or Anointed One, and consecrating him in his mission. As mentioned previously, though a few expected a priestly messiah and others a messianic prophet like Moses, most were looking for an anointed king in the line of David. It seems no one expected Jesus to be what he was—a messiah who was all three at the same time: priest, prophet, and king.

After his baptism, the Spirit led him immediately into the desert to be tempted as Adam was in the Garden and as Israel was in the desert. And Jesus succeeded where both of them failed. Yet his desert victory, though monumental, was not the decisive battle. Luke mentions that, meeting with frustration, Satan retreated—but only for a time (see Luke 4:13).

Jesus then began teaching, healing, and casting out demons in the power of the Spirit. He began gathering the twelve apostles—the future foundation of his Church. As important as all this was, the creed does not mention it. From his Incarnation, the creed leaps directly to what, in the Gospel of Luke, is called his Exodus—his suffering and death "under Pontius Pilate."

The Free Choice of Jesus

Pilate is mentioned because he is actually important in this story of salvation. Jesus' Passion was no mythic event in dream time. It was a real, public event, acted out on the stage of Jewish and Roman history. Pilate was the Roman governor who, in cahoots with the Jewish authorities, had Jesus condemned and executed during Passover, in Jerusalem, most likely in AD 30.[88] He is the representative and voice of "the world" that is at odds with the priorities of God's kingdom.

Jesus was betrayed by Judas, one of the twelve apostles, and was denied by his chief apostle, Peter—abandoned by everyone except the Beloved Disciple John, his mother, and a few other women who stood at the foot of his cross. He was horribly tortured before being marched to Calvary, as if crucifixion itself were not horrible enough.

What all four evangelists make clear is that Jesus knew this was coming and deliberately walked into the trap anyhow. In the Garden of Gethsemane, he could see his captors coming and could have escaped easily. But he held his ground and remained silent as he was falsely accused and then condemned.

Suffering as the Test of Love

The wrong way to understand this is that God's wrath was such that it had to be appeased—that God really had wanted to vent his wrath on us, but Jesus stepped in and took the blow in our place. That misrepresents the

Father entirely. In John 3:16, Jesus claims that the Father had sent him out of his love for the world. Jesus also explains his own actions in terms of love for the Father and the greatest love a man can demonstrate for his friends: to give his life for them.

Jesus had lived a life of perfect obedience and humility up until this point in total love for the Father, his friends, and even his enemies. But could he keep walking steadily in this same path when it was full of painful obstacles? Would he abort his mission after he was betrayed by those closest to him, taunted and mocked by his own people, and brutalized by the pagans, when he found himself facing not only death but excruciating torture?

In the story of Job, we overhear a conversation in which God proudly tells Satan about what a loyal and faithful servant he has in Job. Satan's response is, in effect, "Just let me bring suffering into his life, and you will see how shallow his loyalty really is. ... A little misfortune and he will be cursing you." Fairweather friends are a dime a dozen. Suffering is the true test of love. Job's love had to be put in the crucible to see if it would endure. He passed the test and won from God even greater blessings than he had had before the trial.

Job's life prefigured the life of Christ. Basically, Satan and the corrupt world threw everything they had against Jesus. Physical torture. Shame. Abandonment. Rejection. But none of it could divert him, distract him, or stop him, so relentless was his love. Nothing could provoke him to grumbling or bitterness. He loved his own to the end, as John says (see John 13:1). To the very end.

As Jesus hung on the Cross, a Roman soldier thrust a spear into his side. It pierced his heart, and blood and water flowed out (see John 19:34). Thus, God, who is love, opened his Sacred Heart completely as he gave his life, his own blood, to the very last drop. Poured out in sacrifice, his blood would, thereafter, be consumed under the form of wine in the Eucharist—the sacrament Jesus instituted on the night before he died and which he instructed his apostles to celebrate in memory of him.

And flowing from his side with the blood was the living water, the sign of the Spirit that would soon be given without measure—the life-giving stream the prophets foretold, which would make bitter waters sweet (see Ezekiel 47).

Priest, Prophet, and King

The Cross is Jesus' most eloquent sermon, the supreme revelation that God is love—a love stronger than death. It makes him the last and greatest of God's spokesmen—the prophets. In his death, he is also the perfect king, since a king is a shepherd, and a perfect shepherd is one who lays down his life for his sheep. And he is the ultimate priest, who offers himself as the perfect, unrepeatable sacrifice. As Adam raised his hand to a tree in disobedience, Jesus, the new Adam, raises his in perfect obedience. In this, his final act, he remakes and recapitulates everything, all the way back to the Garden.

He undoes our disobedience by his obedience, our pride by his humility, our selfishness by his love. He does, on our behalf, what we ourselves should have done but could not do.

The Cross itself symbolizes graphically what Jesus' death accomplishes. The vertical beam spans heaven and earth, bringing together God and humanity. On the lateral beam, his arms are stretched out wide, embracing all peoples who are reconciled in him as they are reconciled to God. *At-one-ment* is thus signified and, at the same time, accomplished.

New Adam, New Eve

"The woman" (Genesis 2:23), the mother of all the living (see Genesis 3:20), stood by the tree in the Garden and encouraged Adam in rebellion. Now Mary, the new Eve, stands at the foot of the tree on the hillside, supporting the new Adam in his obedience. To help us understand her role in the drama, Jesus calls his mother "Woman" and then gives her to the disciple closest to his heart so she can be the mother of all those who aspire to be his beloved disciples. At the beginning of the story, at the Annunciation, her faith was demonstrated by her trusting surrender—her *fiat* (Luke 1:38).

It is now manifested as she stands her ground, sharing Jesus' suffering as the lance pierces his heart and, at the same time, her soul (see John 19:25).

Descent into Hell

The Apostles' Creed says, "He descended into hell." One thing to be drawn from this is that Jesus really and truly died. His agony was not an act. The Author of Life experienced death. His soul was separated from his body, and his body was laid in the cold, stone tomb.

But there is more. The actual word used for hell here is not *gehenna*, the hell of the damned, but *hades*, the abode of the dead, including Adam, who awaited liberation from death. The first letter of Peter speaks of Jesus going in the Spirit to preach to the spirits in prison (see 1 Peter 3:19). According to tradition, he did even more, bringing them salvation and freeing them from death. This is depicted in a classic resurrection icon in the Christian East, in which Jesus leads Adam and Eve out of Hades, his cross forming the bridge over the gulf that separates the abode of the dead from the land of the living.

The Resurrection

Though Jesus was condemned as a sinner, his crucifixion was, ironically, a victory over the power of sin. But death, too, had to be conquered. And that was done on Easter morning.

Christ's resurrection is not a quaint, symbolic way of saying that he lives on in the hearts of his disciples—or that he just "came back to life" via resuscitation to return to the life he had before. Resurrection is a necessary and decisive step in Jesus' exodus (see Luke 9:31) as he passes from this world to glory with the Father.

The person who bodily steps out of that tomb is truly Jesus of Nazareth, the same person the disciples walked with for three years. But his humanity has been transformed. It is something new, something that the world has never seen before. He still has the marks of his wounds, and he invites Thomas to probe them, yet he is not recognized by Mary Magdalene, one of his closest followers. He passes through locked doors but proves that he is not a ghost by cooking and eating fish with them (see John 21:1–14).

There are no categories drawn in this world that can adequately describe a reality that is from another world. St. Paul describes it as a "spiritual body," which sounds a little like an oxymoron. The first Adam was a living soul; "the last Adam became a life-giving spirit" (1 Corinthians 15:45).

Most importantly, not only will Jesus live this new risen life in glory forever, never to die again, but, by being fully man, he has made it possible to communicate this new life to us.

The Ascension

The creed leads us to profess that "he ascended into heaven." The Ascension is a much more important part of the story than we often realize. Yes, he goes to prepare a place for us. But he also goes to raise our humanity, which he assumed, to unimaginable heights of glory. His risen humanity, and ours, is glorified at the Father's right hand. And from that vantage point, enthroned above heaven and earth, he can pour out the Advocate, the Gift that will begin to regenerate us, making us sharers in his risen life even now as we continue to walk the dusty roads of this fallen world.

It is not just Jesus' death that saves us. Or just his resurrection. Or just his ascension. It is the entire Passover of Jesus through his life, suffering, death, resurrection, and ascension into glory. The Church calls this entire saving exodus "the paschal mystery."[89] It is the central topic of apostolic preaching and the central event of human history.

Coming as Judge

For the time being, people can either accept Jesus, reject him, or ignore him. Yet a time is coming when this world will draw to a close. His first coming was hidden. His final coming will be sudden and undeniable. At that point, he will be the judge, and the way we have responded in our lifetime to his Word—his invitation to eternal life in him—will be the measure by which we are judged (see John 12:48).

That judgment will simply reveal our own choices to ourselves and everyone else, whether we have loved light or darkness (see John 3:19). And since he is light, those who have loved the light will be drawn to him and be welcomed by him. Those who have chosen darkness will flee from the light. He will be the judge insofar as he will insist that everyone "own" the choices that they have made, which will have become eternal, unchangeable choices at the end of our earthly lives.

Whether the end of the world will come in our lifetime is not known. But what is certain is that each one of us will face the end of his or her own world. At the moment of death, we will meet the judge, and he will honor our choice to accept him, reject him, or ignore him. For that moment of truth, that final exam, we must spend a lifetime of preparation.

Believing in One Lord Jesus Christ

"I believe in one Lord, Jesus Christ," which we profess when we recite the second stanza of the Nicene Creed, means more than believing all the things the creed proclaims about Jesus and his saving work. It means putting our total trust in him and in what he has done for us in the paschal mystery. Faith involves standing on his promises, believing that they are firm enough that we can stake our eternal destiny on them. The Father desires that we be fruitful branches in the true vine (see John 15). So faith's works of love are important and will figure into that "final review" (see Matthew 25:31–46). Yet, at the end of the day, none of us will have given God what he deserves.

But Jesus did. For this reason, it is his righteousness that we will stand on—not our own.[90]

The wind blows where it wills, and you hear the sound of it, but you do not know where it comes from or where it goes; so it is with every one who is born of the Spirit

— *John 3:8*

CHAPTER 9

The Breath of God

Since Jesus is the Son, it is impossible to think of him except in relation to the Father. But the same is true of Jesus' relationship to the Holy Spirit. For Jesus is also the Christ, the Messiah. This means "the one anointed by the Holy Spirit."

The Holy Spirit tends to be the divine Person we think of least. And this is understandable. Jesus is God made visible, and so we have visual images of him, whether it be from the crucifix on our wall or the icon in our prayer corner. And, though the Father is not a male human being, at least "Father" is a human image, and we all crave a father who loves and accepts us as our heavenly Father does. We can imagine both easily.

The Holy Spirit is harder for us to grasp. The dove that descended on Jesus in his baptism is undoubtedly a very meaningful image. But it does not quite move us in the same way as the image of the Sacred Heart or the white-haired Father of the Sistine Chapel.

Nonetheless, Christianity without the Holy Spirit is not Christianity. It is like what Ezekiel saw in his famous vision—a battlefield strewn with dry bones. Jesus came that we might have life and have it more abundantly (see John 10:10). Jesus is the Way, the Truth, and the Life: the Way to the Father, the Truth incarnate, and the source of the Holy Spirit, the Lord and Giver of Life. This third Person of the Holy Trinity is the divine breath that can make corpses come gloriously alive.

God's Breath

The Spirit, like the Church, cannot be understood except through images and analogies. None are adequate, but some are more central than others. A dove can at least be rendered as an object in art, so it tends to be the first image that pops into our minds at the mention of the Holy Spirit. But it is not the primary analogy in Scripture and Tradition.[91]

The Hebrew word for spirit is *ruah*, the word for both breath and wind. This is also the case in Greek (*pneuma*) and Latin (*spiritus*). The reason all these words indicate, at the same time, wind and breath is that the wind is very much like the breath of the world. So the starting point for understanding the Holy Spirit is to recognize him first as the breath of God. Without breath, a body is mere dust and clay (see Genesis 2:7). Breath animates. In John 20:22, the risen Jesus breathes on the disciples and says, "Receive the Holy Spirit."[92]

Breath is also associated with love. God is love, and the term used in theology for the procession of the Holy Spirit within the Trinity is "spiration," or breathing. There is a sigh that human lovers breath. The Spirit is the sigh of divine love between the Father and the Son.[93]

Holy Wind

It is no accident that the coming of the first sign of the Spirit's presence at Pentecost was a mighty wind. Wind can blow like a gentle breeze and whisper in a still, small voice (see 1 Kings 19:12). Or it can arrive in gale-force strength as it did at Pentecost (see Acts 2:2). You cannot really see it. But you can often see its effects.

What is always true about wind is that you cannot control it. It is oscillating and elusive. Sometimes it rises, and sometimes it falls. The Spirit, like the wind, is free. And he makes those who follow him free. This freedom of the Holy Wind and its children was pointed out by Jesus to Nicodemus: "The wind blows where it wills, and you hear the sound of it, but you do not know where it comes from or where it goes; so it is with every one who is born of the Spirit" (John 3:8).

Jesus, the Lion of Judah, resists those who would seek to tame him. His Holy Wind likewise refuses to be domesticated. There is something wild about the Son and his Spirit.

The Lord and Giver of Life

The title given to the Spirit in the Nicene Creed is "the Lord, the giver of Life."

In the work of creation, the Spirit or Breath of God is the giver of biological life (*bios*), which is a wonderful thing. He is also the giver of distinctively human life (*psyche*), which is still more wonderful (see Genesis 2:7 and Isaiah 42:5).[94] In the work of redemption, the Spirit is the Lord and giver of supernatural, eternal life (*zoe*), which is of another order of life entirely.[95] Eternal life is not simply different in *duration* from mortal life, in that it does not end. No, it is different in *quality*. In and through the Holy Spirit, it is God's own Trinitarian life that is poured out and offered to us, that we may become "partakers of the divine nature" (2 Peter 1:4). God's love, the love stronger than death, demonstrated most perfectly by Christ on the Cross, is poured out into our hearts through the Holy Spirit who has been given to us (see Romans 5:5).

Living Water

This description of the Spirit as "poured out" brings up another key image of the Spirit taught by Jesus. If anything besides breath is associated with life, it is water. Human beings can last quite a while without food. But nothing endures very long without water. In the dry, blistering heat of the Holy Land, the image is even more telling.[96]

The Holy Spirit is not just water, but living water—moving, invigorating, alive with refreshment, slaking thirst forever. Not only does such water not run out—it multiplies. When a person drinks it, this mysterious water becomes a spring within the drinker that wells up to eternal life (see John 4:13–14). The partaker goes on to become a source of this water: "Out of his heart shall flow rivers of living water" (John 7:38).

Jesus precedes his disciples in all things. When his heart was pierced with the lance (see John 19:34), it became the first source of the saving stream foretold by the prophets (see Ezekiel 47:1–12; Zechariah 13:1; 14:8) and by Jesus himself, the final and perfect prophet. If we open our hearts to him and drink of the living water flowing from his Sacred Heart, that water will flow from our hearts as well, slaking the thirst of a parched world.

Promise of the Father

When Jesus spoke of rivers of living water streaming from the hearts of those who believed in him, the Evangelist followed his words with an editorial comment: "Now this he said about the Spirit, which those who believed in him were to receive; for *as yet the Spirit had not been given, because Jesus was not yet glorified*" (John 7:39; emphasis added).

Everything in Jesus' ministry was done in the power of the Spirit by whom he was conceived and with whom he was anointed. It was "by the finger of God," the Holy Spirit, that he cast out demons. It was by the Lord, the Giver of Life, that he healed the sick and raised the dead. The holy breath inspired the words by which Jesus taught the multitudes.

It is apparent, however, that throughout his public ministry, his closest disciples did not quite "get it." There were flashes of insight, like Peter's at Caesarea Philippi. But the twelve were slow to understand and even slower to believe, even after the resurrection of Jesus, when they scoffed at the news brought by the women (see Luke 24:11). They showed the same dullness of mind and hardness of heart that we see in the entire history of Israel in Scripture. This is what it means when John says that the Spirit had not yet been given.

When, forty days after the Resurrection, Jesus was about to take his final leave, he told the disciples to pray for the "promise of the Father" (Acts 1:4). He identified this promise with being baptized with and immersed in the Holy Spirit (see Acts 1:5). He described this also in terms of receiving "power" (Acts 1:8).

He had spoken to them about the kingdom of God throughout his ministry and had demonstrated its power in signs and wonders. He had spoken of it during the forty days of his resurrection appearances among them (see Acts 1:3). But they still did not get it. They asked if now was the time that the kingdom would be restored to Israel, as in the days of David or Solomon. They still misunderstood the kingdom in political and nationalistic terms (see Acts 1:6).

In essence, Jesus said, "Forget about that." The promises are not about that. The fulfillment of the promise is a Person. The Kingdom of God is the work of that Person.

So they returned to the Upper Room and spent nine days in prayer, together with Mary (see Acts 1:14). This was the first novena. Every novena since, no matter what outward form it takes, asks for the same thing as this one: the coming of God's kingdom, for which the Lord taught us to pray (see Matthew 6:10).

When Pentecost came, the Holy Wind came upon them like a thunderclap. It moved the gathered community to leave the place where they were gathered, spilling onto the streets of Jerusalem and, in the years to come, onto the highways and byways of the Roman world (see Acts 2).

The Wind, who is also the Living Water, appeared on this occasion as tongues of fire. Fire gives warmth and gives light. It also consumes, cleanses, purifies, and transforms whatever it touches.[97]

What we see on that first Pentecost is an explosion of joy, praise, and courage. The disciples who ran away from the Garden of Gethsemane in fear now run into the streets, risking their lives to tell others the glad tidings—that the promises have been fulfilled.

Luke wrote both the Gospel that bears his name and the book of Acts. At this point in Acts, he introduces a word that he did not associate with the disciples before Pentecost. But now it becomes a constant refrain as he describes the way they operate. That word is *parrhesia,* or "boldness."[98]

What has changed? How is this the fulfillment of the promises? Jesus is Emmanuel, God *with us.* The Holy Spirit is God *with-in us.* The old Law written in stone together with the new Law preached in the Beatitudes is at last inscribed in people's hearts (see Jeremiah 31:33; Ezekiel 36:26–29). The Holy Fire melts the hearts of stone and transforms them into hearts of flesh. The Holy Breath revives and animates them. The River of Living Water makes their souls fertile so that fruits of jubilation and mutual love can be borne in abundance (see Acts 2:43–47). The Holy Wind empowers them from within, driving them into the streets, impelling them at last to obey God and not men (see Acts 5:29). The disciples go on to heal as Jesus healed, and many of them suffer as Jesus suffered. The same unstoppable love we see in him, we now see in them—because the Spirit, who is Love, finally dwells within them.

Jesus is the truth. After Pentecost, the Holy Spirit empowers the disciples to understand that truth (see John 16:12–13). Jesus is the life. The Spirit now plants that life in the depth of their souls. Jesus is the way. The Spirit now propels them courageously on that way.

The Sanctifier

God is the source of holiness. Only he can sanctify. Keeping in mind that the three Persons always act together in unison, it is nonetheless the case that they act together each according to their personal properties. The Spirit is called the Holy Spirit because he, in a preeminent way, is the Sanctifier, the one who penetrates to the depth of our being and transforms us from within to share in the divine nature (see 2 Peter 1:4).

Here, we have to correct a misconception that we often find among Christians: Jesus did not die simply so that our guilt would be wiped from God's record book on high. Surely, we are acquitted and made righteous through Christ. But, more importantly, we are changed. Jesus' death, resurrection, and ascension give him the power and authority to send the Spirit to scour sin from our hearts. This interior cleansing, making us sharers in Christ's righteousness, is in a special way the work of the Spirit.

As the Advocate or Paraclete, the Holy Spirit is our defense lawyer.[99] He gently prompts us to be honest before the judgment seat of God and plead guilty to our sins. In contrast, the word "devil" (*diabolos*) comes from the word "accuser." The Devil either tortures us with our guilt, telling us that we are no good, or urges us to foolishly deny all charges. The Holy Spirit is on our side, which is literally what "Advocate" means. From that position, he gently nudges us to "fess up," admit our sins, and entrust ourselves to the mercy of the Judge. He gives us the strength to let go and open our hearts to mercy. In fact, he is mercy in person.

Jesus said, "No one can come to me unless the Father who sent me draws him" (John 6:44). The Holy Spirit is that magnetic force that the Father uses to attract us to his Son. But the Holy Spirit, who is free, will never compromise our freedom. His prompting to repent is that still small voice, that gentle breeze that does not overpower. His promptings can be resisted. And that is why Jesus says that blaspheming, or resisting, the Holy Spirit is the unforgivable sin (see Mark 3:28–30; Matthew 12:31–32). Closing our hearts to him is closing ourselves off from mercy. And God ultimately will respect those who say no to his mercy. There is no one in hell except those who choose it. Those who go to heaven are those who say to God, "Thy will be done." Those who go to hell are those to whom God says, "Thy will be done."[100]

The Gift

The word *grace* is one that all Christians have heard often. It means literally a gift that is given "gratis," or freely. The Holy Spirit is uncreated grace. He is the free "Gift that contains all gifts."[101] He gently prompts us to turn our backs on sin, turn toward Christ, and begin walking. These are the gifts of repentance and faith. Once we say yes to Christ through faith, grace takes up residence within and changes us.

We were made in the image and likeness of God. But through our first parents' decision, which we ratify by our own sins, God's likeness was lost. Sin makes us unlike God. Uncreated grace begins to refashion God's likeness in us, restoring our beauty as a son or daughter, making us like God again as well as pleasing to him. This transformation is an ongoing process of "divinization," coming more and more to share "the divine nature" (2 Peter 1:4). The Spirit is sculpting us, progressively making us something ever more beautiful for God. In Eastern Christianity, this is called *theosis*. In Latin Christianity, it is called *sanctification*. The end product is described in the Beatitudes (see Matthew 5:1–11) and embodied in the saints.

Virtues

The Gift contains, within himself, varied kinds of gifts.

The first and most important thing the Spirit brings with his coming are the greatest gifts—the gifts that last: faith, hope, and love (see 1 Corinthians 13:13). We have already spoken of faith. We spoke of it at the outset of this book because it is the gateway to all other good things. Hope and love we will discuss in greater detail in Part III. For now, suffice it to say that these three are the essence of holiness. Holiness is not to be identified with any particular state of life but rather with the perfection of these three virtues[102] in whatever vocation people find themselves.

The word *virtue* really connotes the idea of strength or power. The virtues are, in a sense, spiritual muscles. They are given by the Spirit as free gifts. We receive our physical muscles also as free gifts. But for them to get us where we want to go, our muscles must be fed and exercised. In this process of nourishment, training, and development, the Holy Spirit is our personal trainer, who not only directs but empowers our program of development.

The Spirit's Seven Gifts

The seven gifts of the Holy Spirit are mentioned in Isaiah 11. They are like seven antennas by which we become capable of picking up the signals of the Holy Spirit as he gently leads us to the heights of holiness—the perfection of faith, hope, and love.[103]

Wisdom is a foretaste, in this life, of the life to come. We often associate it with contemplation—the experience of mystics. But it is a gift for all, even if many Christians never take this gift out of its wrapping paper. This gift is activated most often by the ardent pursuit of God in prayer. By the gift of *understanding*, the Holy Spirit causes an inner light bulb to turn on, so we can understand God's word intimately. Look at the difference between the obtuseness of the Twelve during the public ministry of Jesus and the brilliant insight of St. Paul after his conversion, and you will see what the gift of understanding does. By the gift of *knowledge,* even the simplest can discern the difference between something that is in accord with the gospel and what is not. The gift of *counsel* is supernatural guidance. *Fortitude* ("might") is the kind of supernatural boldness and courage we see after Pentecost. *Piety* is an attraction, affection, and reverence for all that is associated with our heavenly Father. *Fear of the Lord* is an inner aversion to anything that would displease our Father or risk separating us from him.

Charisms

The seven gifts are primarily given to us, says St. Thomas Aquinas, to build us up personally, perfecting us in holiness. The charisms, on the other hand, are gifts given to individual members of the body of Christ for the building up of the entire body. A few are associated with vocations; celibacy and marriage are spoken of as charisms by St. Paul (see 1 Corinthians 7). Through the sacrament of Holy Orders, a gift of the Spirit for the sake of building up the body is given to bishops, priests, and deacons.[104]

But the rest of the charisms are freely given by the Spirit to the faithful. They can be rather spectacular, such as healing, miracles, tongues, and prophecy, or seemingly mundane, such as teaching, hospitality, and administration. They are not just natural gifts. Even the latter few, though very human realities, are "graced" and transformed by the Spirit. Someone with the charism of hospitality helps the guest to experience the Father's love as if he or she were in the Father's house. Someone with a charismatic gift of teaching the Faith leaves the student feeling not simply informed but deeply touched by God and inwardly enlightened.[105]

The Fruits of the Spirit

The fruits of the Spirit, described by St. Paul in Galatians 5:22–23, are love, joy, peace, patience, kindness, goodness, faithfulness, gentleness, and self-control. This is much like Jesus' description of the Beatitudes in the Sermon on the Mount (see Matthew 5:1–11) and Paul's description of love in 1 Corinthians 13. And it is in terms of this fruit of the Spirit that Paul describes the kingdom of God: "The kingdom of God does not mean food and drink but righteousness and peace and joy in the Holy Spirit" (Romans 14:17).

It is no accident that it is in the Last Supper discourse of St. John, where Jesus teaches the most on the Holy Spirit, that Jesus uses the metaphor of the vine and branches to make clear that the thing the Father desires most is that we bear much fruit (see John 15:1–17). If we are the branches, Jesus the vine, and the Father the vinedresser, then the vital sap that makes the branches bear fruit is the same Holy Spirit who brought forth from Mary the blessed fruit of her womb.

CHAPTER 10

The Spirit and the Bride

The recitation of the creed is an act of entrusting ourselves completely and without reserve to the Trinity. The faith we profess is a dynamic movement into the Triune God. For this reason, we have seen that both the Apostles' and the Nicene Creeds have three stanzas, one for each person of the Trinity. "I believe in the Father ... in the Son ... in the Holy Spirit."

But then we continue. In the Nicene Creed, we say, "I believe in one, holy, catholic and apostolic Church." So does that mean that there is a fourth stanza to the Creed? Do we believe in the Church as we do in God?

Believing the Church

The problem boils down to the limitations inherent in the English language.[106] When you profess the creed in Latin or Greek, the original languages of the Apostles' and Nicene Creeds, respectively, it is easy to see the answer to this question. The creeds read, "I believe *in* the Father. ... I believe *in* the Son. ... I believe *in* the Holy Spirit." And then both creeds say, "I believe *the Church*." Not "in the Church." This is deliberate and is meant to communicate something very important. All the ancient commentators on the creed point this out and explain it. So does the *Catechism*.[107]

To God and to God alone do we give our hearts in the act of faith. On him alone do we rely for our salvation. In this sense, we only believe *in* or *into* him. Catholic teaching is clear: it would be idolatrous to entrust ourselves to the Church in this same way. To do so would also mean to set ourselves up for crushing disillusionment. Perhaps the reason Jesus chose weak men like Peter, Judas, and Thomas as his first disciples was to try to make this clear to us right from the start.

No, there is no fourth stanza to the creed. The article on the Church is part of the creed's profession of faith in the work of the Spirit, just as the Cross and Resurrection are part of the creed's profession of faith in the work of Christ.

Here is what we are saying when we say in English, "I believe in the holy catholic Church." It means *we believe that the Church is no mere human institution.* True, the Church includes many people who are "works in progress," who fail and fail terribly. Yet we believe it is, nonetheless, a work of the Holy Spirit. He brought it to birth on the day of Pentecost, and he has sustained it ever since. We are saying we believe in the Holy Spirit working in and through the Church, despite the human frailty of its members and leaders.

Another way to explain the meaning of this line is like this: *I believe the Church in its testimony to Jesus.* Simon was weak, but when at Caesarea Philippi the Lord asked, "Who do *you* say that I am?" Peter blurted out, "You are the Christ, the son of the living God!" (Matthew 16:15–16; emphasis added). Jesus praised this and attributed this bold statement to God's revelation (see Matthew 16:17). Peter's official testimony to Jesus was spot on. Prompted by the Spirit, it can be trusted. Peter's subsequent private advice to Jesus to avoid the Cross was prompted not by the Spirit but by the flesh, and Jesus rebuked him for it. Both sides of the reality of the Church are shown here—the reliability of its testimony to Christ and the weakness of its members and pastors. We trust the Church in its witness to the Savior; we do not rely on the Church as our savior.

There is one additional way to understand the relationship between the Church and our faith: *I believe within the Church.* Faith is a personal act, but it is not an isolated and purely individual act (see CCC 166). As the Bride of Christ, the Church is the great corporate believer. The early Church saw the "I do" of the baptismal promises as akin to wedding vows. So my personal profession of faith, the giving of my heart to Christ, his Father, and his Spirit, is a participation in the one faith of the one Bride. It is the Church—the Bride of Christ, as it were—speaking through me, saying, "I do."[108]

Faith does not come out of nowhere. It comes from hearing the Word of God that someone announces to us (see Romans 10:17). The Easter Vigil dramatically illustrates how Faith is a light that is passed on from one believer to another within the community of the Church. At the start of the Vigil Mass, the Church building is dark, and the congregation waits expectantly in silence, each person holding an unlit candle. The Easter candle is then processed into the church. A few candles are lit from the Easter candle and their owners begin passing the light to other candles around them. As the light spreads throughout the church, it is reflected in the faces of the believers.

This calls to mind another of the great symbols for the Church in Scripture and Tradition: the Church as our mother. The baptismal font is the womb of our mother, the Church, made fruitful and life-giving by the power of the Holy Spirit. Once we are born, our mother teaches us the language of faith.[109] As St. Cyprian so famously put it, "He cannot have God for his father who has not the Church for his mother."[110]

Church as a Sacrament

At this juncture, it is important to explain further what it means that the Church is a mystery. We find the term *mystery* in the New Testament on the lips of both Jesus and St. Paul. The Lord speaks about the mystery of the kingdom of God (see Mark 4:11; Matthew 13:13[111]). Paul speaks of the mystery of God several times in his first letter to the Corinthians and then goes on to describe himself and his fellow apostles as "stewards of the mysteries of God.[112]

These references have this in common: They apply to something visible through which God's invisible grace and power are at work in a hidden way. It takes God's revelation and faith in that revelation to recognize what is really in play here. The miracles of Jesus are called "signs" in John's Gospel for this very reason. There is more to them than meets the eye. Each miracle is a marvel in itself, but it points beyond itself to something still more marvelous. There are wonderful events and people throughout salvation history—the Exodus, the manna, Moses, David—that are all preparing for something and foreshadowing something. There is a mysterious, divine purpose working in and through all these persons, places, and events.

The Greek word *mysterion*, which describes this invisible purpose of God working under and through the visible, was translated into Latin and English in two different terms: mystery (*mysterium*) and sacrament (*sacramentum*). "Mystery" is better at communicating the idea that what God is doing here surpasses our understanding. "Sacrament" gets across better the idea of something visible that God uses as an instrument to transmit his invisible grace—his powerful love that comes to save and transform.

The very first and original sacrament is the humanity of Jesus Christ. It makes visible the invisible God and is the instrument of divine power that flows through him to teach, bless, and heal.[113] After the Ascension and Pentecost, the ecclesial[114] Body of Christ, the Church, now fulfills the role of the Lord's physical body as the primary sacrament. It is the visible instrument through which God's grace is hidden and through which his saving grace flows. Through his ecclesial body, the Lord Jesus continues to touch, bless, heal, and sanctify.

So the Church has a visible dimension: a hierarchical structure, visible rites, catechism classes, canon law, and charitable ministries. All these things anyone can see. But beneath it all and beyond it all is something invisible that we can only perceive by faith: God's grace working through it all and the bonds of faith, hope, and love between believers and God, forged by the Holy Spirit. The visible exists for the sake of the invisible. We need always to keep this priority in mind. Yet we also need to resist the temptation, in moments of frustration, to walk away from the Church in its visible and institutional dimension. For in God's dispensation, the visible is the indispensable vehicle for his invisible work. The visible is both a sign and an instrument of what it is all about: reconciliation and communion with God and with one another.

The Church Is One

The Apostles' Creed speaks of "the holy catholic Church." In its description of the Church, the Nicene Creed adds two more adjectives: "one" and "apostolic." These four qualities—one, holy, catholic, and apostolic—are known as the "Marks" or "Notes of the Church." They encapsulate the essence of its nature. Pondering them is a great way to understand what the Church is really about.

First of all, the Church of Christ is *one*. Christ does not have multiple bodies. He has a Bride, not a harem.

Sin divides. Love unites. Salvation is all about communion.[115] The Trinity is a unity—an eternal mystery of intimate communion. God has opened his heart to us, inviting us to share in his inner life of love. Jesus prayed the night before he died that we, his Church, would be one even as he and the Father are one (see John 17:11). The unity of the Church is a participation in and a sign of the unity of the Trinity.

There is a missionary urgency that requires the Church to make this unity a perceptible, recognizable reality. Our testimony that Jesus is Lord is only credible to the extent that we are one. Jesus says this twice during what is known as his "high priestly prayer" at the close of the Last Supper. The second time he mentions it, he asks the Father that "they may become perfectly one, so that the world may know that you have sent me" (John 17:23). The more imperfect our unity, the harder it is for the world to know that Jesus is the One sent by God.

Despite all the schisms and separations that have occurred over its two-thousand-year history, the Church has not lost the unity that is an indispensable quality of who she is. Some have deliberately walked away from this unity. Some have been driven away by scandal. Some have, through no fault of their own, been born into communities that have been separated from full communion with the Church. Some are visibly united to that Church and fully incorporated into it sacramentally, yet they are not one with it because they reject revealed doctrine or stubbornly cling to mortal sin.

All these things wound the Church's unity in this world but do not destroy it. The disunity does, however, set up a scandal and stumbling block in the way of those who need Christ but do not yet know him.

Everyone must strive to "maintain the unity of the Spirit in the bond of peace" (Ephesians 4:3). We are to preserve and strengthen the unity that exists and to be reconcilers and healers where that bond has been wounded. "Blessed are the peacemakers, for they shall be called sons of God" (Matthew 5:9). Perhaps not all of us are equipped to engage in dialogue about doctrinal differences. But all can be bridge builders. An Orthodox priest friend of mine once told me that the wall between our communions went up one brick at a time. Each one of us can be responsible for walking up to that wall and pulling off a brick. Our prayers for unity and our efforts to love and understand fellow Christians of other confessions can make a difference.

But what about Christians of other confessions? If the Church is one, can they be saved?

The bonds of unity in the Church are both visible and invisible. Faith, hope, and love are invisible. Sacramental incorporation into the Church through Baptism, Confirmation, and the Eucharist, along with submission to the bishops and pope—these are visible bonds. Sadly, some are fully incorporated and on parish rosters but, through sin and formal heresy, can be far from communion in faith, hope, and love. On the other hand, many who are not canonically reckoned as Catholics are intimately united with the heart of the Church through zealous faith, intense hope, and lively charity. Some of them have even been visibly incorporated into the one Church through valid Baptism. They are in communion with the Catholic Church visibly and invisibly, though imperfectly so.

And there are people who are not baptized but who love and seek God or at least love and seek the truth. This seeking and openness is in many cases a sign that they, in a hidden way, have responded to the Spirit who is drawing them to Christ. Even these, according to the teaching of the Church, are in some way ordered toward or related to the community of salvation.[116]

Our job is to be as perfectly and fully united to the one Church as we can possibly be and to share the fullness of the riches of Christ with all, helping to bring each and every person in our lives one step closer to full unity with the one Church.

The Church as Holy

In light of the obvious failings of many high-profile Catholics, whether they be cardinals or statesmen, one must ask: In what way can we call the Church holy?

First, the entire goal of the Church in this world is the glorification of God and the sanctification of his people. In a sense, these twin goals are one and the same, for the glory of God is the sanctified human being.[117] So everything about the Church's life, all its liturgies and ministries, are ultimately ordered to this end. The Church is holy because it is a creation of the Holy Spirit, because its goal is to make people holy, and because it has been entrusted with all the means of grace and sanctification to do so. This is the Church as objectively holy.

Subjectively, each member of the body must make the decision not only to preserve the holiness that he or she received in Baptism but to increase it and make it bear abundant fruit (see Matthew 13:1–23; 25:14–30). Some throw away the gift; others barely preserve it with no increase; and some yield thirty-fold, some sixty, and some one-hundred-fold. In every generation, there are those who bear fruit abundantly and often do so heroically in the face of hardship and opposition. Most of these are known only to a few and, of course, to God. Some are publicly canonized by the Church, which is to say recognized to be with God in heaven after living a life of extraordinary virtue.

In Mary and the saints, the Church is completely holy subjectively as well as objectively. The communion of saints glorified in heaven is the Bride without spot or blemish. The thing we often forget is that, after two thousand years of saints and martyrs, the Church in glory may very well include more than the Church on earth, which is always a work in progress.

That many choose mediocrity over heroic faithfulness is not surprising. All of us are aware of the constant temptation to lukewarmness and compromise.

What is startling is just how consistently, in every generation, the Church has produced extraordinary heroes. This begins with the apostles, who despite their rather unpromising start, became a brigade that turned the world upside down. St. Francis of Assisi, St. Teresa of Calcutta (Mother Teresa), the teenaged Joan of Arc, who turned the tide of a hundred-year war in a matter of two weeks—these and thousands more equally remarkable people from every nation and historical era prove that the Church is, in fact, holy and capable of making holy the simplest and earthliest of human beings. By taking full advantage of the means of grace made available by the Holy Church, many have risen to the heights of sanctity.[118]

The Church as Catholic

We examined the term "catholic" in Chapter Two. Here we would just like to reflect a little further on catholicity as universality that includes and embraces all.

In our discussion of creation, we already noted the way God works. God is a unity in diversity—one divine nature possessed equally by three irreducibly unique Persons. The entire natural world reflects this in an ecosystem that is a wonder of unity in a kaleidoscope of diverse species. This is true in the human society of the Church as well; the unity we see is characterized not by a monotonous conformity but by a richness of diversity. In western society, it is part of our cultural inheritance that a person is a free subject with inviolable dignity—unique and irreplaceable. This notion of personhood actually came into western culture from the theology of the Trinity.[119]

So the unity of the Church is not the unity of communism or fascism, which is bought at the price of human dignity, freedom, and individual uniqueness. The authentic unity brought about by the Holy Spirit is like the unity of the ecosystem created by him, or the unity of the human body—unique and diverse parts working together in wonderful harmony.

The Church is an ordered community with different hierarchical roles played by bishops, priests, and deacons. There are members of canonically recognized religious communities where members take vows of poverty, chastity, and obedience. There are others who live these same "evangelical counsels" without being members of such communities. The diversity of lifestyles among formally recognized communities is amazing: There are solitary hermits like the Carthusians, monks and nuns who live a contemplative life in community like Benedictines and Cistercians, and active religious like Mother Teresa's Missionaries of Charity.

The diversity of lay ministries, apostolates, movements, and communities is breathtaking. Every culture, every personality type, and every temperament is represented.

The Catholic Church is actually a communion of Churches. The largest, the Western Church, is usually what we in the West think of when we think "Catholic." But there are twenty-two Eastern Catholic Churches, each with a unique and equally Catholic spiritual and liturgical tradition. Their services and particular traditions are of a different style than those of the Western or "Latin" Church. Their modes of devotion are a little different. Their liturgical calendars differ. Their canon law also differs from the Western code.

Yet these Churches, usually led by a patriarch or major archbishop, are one in faith and sacraments, and are in full communion with each other. The invisible bond of that unity is the Holy Spirit. The visible touch stone of that unity is the successor of St. Peter, the pope. To be in communion with him, the bishop of Rome, is to be in communion with the Catholic Church throughout the world. As Peter stood on Pentecost day and served as the spokesman of the apostles,[120] so the pope today is the visible center and spokesman of the successors of the apostles.[121]

The Church as Apostolic

This leads to the final note of the Church: the Church as apostolic. The apostles are the foundation of the Church, the new Jerusalem (See Ephesians 2:20–22; Revelation 21:14). From them come the apostolic Scriptures and the apostolic Tradition, which bring us the Word of God. So the Church as "apostolic" means first of all that it is founded on apostolic truth.

But the apostles ordained successors, imparting the gift of the Holy Spirit by the laying on of hands. It is the continual, unbroken, personal link of this succession that guarantees the Church's faithful transmission of apostolic truth. So the Church is apostolic also in preserving the apostolic structure established by Jesus and the personal, historical link joining the successors of the apostles today to Peter, Andrew, James, John, Paul, Barnabas, and all those called apostles in the New Testament.

There is a final way that the Church is apostolic. Apostle means "one who is sent." The Church is essentially missionary, charged by Christ to "make disciples of all nations" (Matthew 28:19) and bring Christ's truth and love to a needy world. While the successors of the apostles preside over the Church's mission, every baptized and confirmed Christian is called to participate in the apostolic work of communicating Christ to the world.[122]

Baptism and the Forgiveness of Sins

After the mention of the Church and its essential characteristics, the Nicene Creed notes that we "believe in one baptism for the forgiveness of sins." The Apostles' Creed renders this "the communion of saints and the forgiveness of sins."

Here we stop and remember that originally the creed was taught to new Christians just a few days before their Baptism, when each of them would publicly profess it. In the early Church, the extensive preparation before Baptism did not include very much instruction on all the sacraments. The reason for this is that the sacraments are mysteries that can only be truly understood by new Christians after they have been enlightened in Baptism with the Spirit's gift of understanding. The entire week following Baptism was a week of intensive instruction on the rest of the sacraments, which we will treat in Part III of this book. This is why the Nicene Creed mentions only Baptism. But one of Baptism's key effects is mentioned in both creeds: the forgiveness of sins. Baptism reconciles us to God. Through this sacrament, the crushing burden of guilt is lifted off our backs by the one who bore our burdens.

There is only one Baptism. Unlike the Jews of Jesus' day who took ritual baths frequently, sometimes even more than once a day, Christian Baptism cleanses us through the once-and-for-all sacrifice that takes away all sin (see Acts 2:38; 22:16). Sometimes a person is baptized as a child and later wishes to make a serious commitment to Christ. Or someone sins seriously after Baptism and wishes to come back the Christ and his Church. In both cases, a person is not re-baptized, since there is only one Baptism for the forgiveness of sins. Rather, a person renews his or her baptismal promises through the sacrament of Penance, which we will discuss further in Part III.

The Communion of Saints

Instead of mentioning Baptism specifically, as the Nicene Creed does when it mentions the forgiveness of sins, the Apostles' Creed instead professes that we "believe in the communion of saints and the forgiveness of sins."

The primary and original meaning of the communion of saints is a communion in holy things, meaning "the mysteries of God" (1 Corinthians 4:1), namely, the Word of God and the sacraments, including Baptism. The riches of Christ are a shared family inheritance. This communion in holy things creates a bond among us, a communion of saints in the sense of holy people. This communion is unbreakable because the bond is the divine and eternal Person of the Holy Spirit. Even death cannot break it. So we who are still fighting the good fight on earth are intimately united with the members of the body who are already in glory. The glorified saints pray for us. And we, likewise, are united with and pray for those beloved deceased who are still undergoing final purification, or what is called purgatory. Those who die in a state of grace and communion with God may still be imperfectly purified from attachment to sin. Purgatory is the process of purification necessary to enter the joy of heaven (see CCC 1030–1032).

There is a powerful solidarity and sharing of spiritual goods among all the members of Christ regardless of where we may be. "If one member suffers, all suffer together; if one member is honored, all rejoice together" (1 Corinthians 12:26). St. Thérèse of Lisieux, the Little Flower, said, shortly before her death, "I will spend my heaven doing good on earth."[123]

PART III

Our Life

Three times were
you plunged in the
water and came forth,
signifying Christ's
burial for three days.

— *St. Cyril of Jerusalem*

CHAPTER 11

Liturgy and Sacraments

Jesus came that we may "have life, and have it abundantly" (John 10:10). The creed's final stanza, centering on the Lord and Giver of Life, ends by affirming the glorious resurrection of the body and life everlasting.

But how does the Holy Spirit impart the life of Christ to us here and now? How does he give us, even now, a foretaste of that life to come?

Liturgy

Jesus is our head in all things, including prayer. He is the eternal high priest, who has ascended to God's right hand, who never ceases to give praise and thanks to the Father. And he never ceases interceding for us. The glorified saints and the angels join him in this perpetual praise and intercession. The Church on earth, through its public and official prayer, joins Christ and the saints in this heavenly worship, which we call "liturgy" (see CCC 1069).

Through the liturgy, the whole people of God, led by Christ our head, are swept up in the worship of God. Through the power of the Spirit, the paschal mystery of Christ is made present so that we can draw life from it and enter into it more fully.

The seven sacraments are the central heartbeat of the liturgy—most especially the Eucharist. But the liturgy of the Church also includes the Liturgy of the Hours as the prayer of Christ united with his body, the Church.

One way we experience the liturgy is in the rhythm of the liturgical seasons and the memorials of the saints. Another is in the use of sacramentals, the Church's blessings, which dispose us to receive the grace of the sacraments.

The most important thing to know about the liturgy is that nothing else in the Church's life surpasses it in excellence or importance. This is because liturgical prayers are priestly acts of Christ, the High Priest, united with all the members of his body.[124] In the liturgy, Christ and the whole Church— on earth as well as in heaven—are present. Whether it is a penitent and priest in confession, someone reciting the Morning Prayer alone at home, or the pope celebrating Mass with thousands in attendance, the liturgy is extremely powerful. It is our participation in that heavenly worship before God's throne that we glimpse throughout the book of Revelation (see Revelation 5:4–10; 7:9–17; 11:17–18).

This is not to say that other forms of devotional prayer, like the Rosary, are unimportant. No. The liturgy is the source and summit of our faith and life, celebrating and strengthening our bonds of love in an incomparable way. This is the point of all other activities, devotions, and ministries: Everything in the Christian life is ordered to communion with God and one another. All the energy to serve and evangelize flows from this communion. The liturgy is the power source that enables us to ascend to the heights of holiness and bring others along with us. It is primarily by means of the liturgy that we attach ourselves to the vine who is Christ so that the living sap of the Holy Spirit can make us yield abundant fruit.[125]

What do we mean when we say that the liturgy is the source and summit of the life of the Church?[126] Imagine the Christian life as a mountain tall enough to have a snow-capped summit. At the lower base of the snowy cap are the celebrations of the liturgical year, the Liturgy of the Hours, and the Church's blessings. Above them are the sacraments, and at the very pinnacle of the mountain is the Eucharist. Melting snow runs down the mountainside, forever watering the entire mountain. This is what it means for the liturgy to be both the summit and the source of the life of the Church.

Sacraments

When the Word became flesh in Jesus, the humanity of Christ made visible the invisible God. His grace flowed through his words, which people could hear with their ears. It flowed through his gestures, which people could see with their eyes. It also flowed through his touch and his embrace. And sometimes he used earthy, material objects to serve as vehicles of his invisible power. When healing the man born blind, he made a paste of mud, anointed the man's eyes, and then told the man to wash in the pool of Siloam (see John 9:6–7). These are figures of the entire sacramental order as God uses perceptible signs to reveal his truth and transmit his love and his life to us.

The early Church sometimes used the word "mystery" to refer to the sacraments (see CCC 1115), which offers a distinct connotation.[127] As mystery, a sacrament is a visible sign of an invisible grace. This is why the sacraments are full of visible gestures and symbols: water, perfumed oil, the laying on of hands, and bread and wine. As with the Incarnation, God offers us his spiritual truth and life and love through physical means.

The word *sacrament* has yet another powerful connotation. In the Roman army, a *sacramentum* was a ceremony during which a military oath of loyalty was sworn. The commander committed himself to take care of the soldier, and the soldier swore loyalty to the commander and the legion unto death. The sacraments of the New Covenant are covenant oaths whereby Christ pledges to bless and save us and each of us renews our covenant of loyalty to Christ and his Body.

In the ancient and biblical world, covenants established family bonds.[128] People entered into and renewed their life in the covenant through various ritual words and ritual actions (e.g., circumcision). Covenants were typically formed through oaths, sacrifices, and a communion meal.

The New Covenant, established by Jesus Christ, follows this same pattern, with Baptism as the entrance into the covenant and the Eucharist as the ongoing renewal of this sacred covenant. The sacraments become the sacred "oaths" by which we unite ourselves to God and he to us; the sacraments are the sacred ritual actions by which we enter into and renew our life in the family of God—the Church.[129]

Many ceremonies and rituals have been passed down through Scripture and Tradition. Gradually, it became clear that seven of them stood apart from the rest because they were instituted by Christ himself.[130] Some were instituted by his explicit words, like the command to go and baptize all nations (see Matthew 28:19) or, on the night before he died, to "do this in remembrance of me" (see 1 Corinthians 11:24; Luke 22:19). Sometimes their institution is more implicit. Based on Jesus' words and actions during his earthly ministry, their full meaning became clear later on—as for example regarding marriage, when Jesus referred to himself as "the bridegroom" (Mark 2:19; Luke 5:34), performed his first public sign at a wedding celebration (see John 2:1–11), and restored marriage to God's original intent as something indissoluble (see Matthew 19:8).

While God's presence and power can reach us in many ways (e.g., through prayer, the Word of God, and the encounter with Christ in the poor), the seven sacraments are our privileged encounters with the Risen Christ; each offers a distinct grace and embrace of the Father through the Son and in the Spirit.

Baptism

Baptism is the gateway to the Christian life. It represents—and brings about—a new birth into divine life by incorporating us into the paschal mystery. In Baptism, we are plunged into Jesus' death and resurrection (see Romans 6:3–4). St. Cyril of Jerusalem explains the meaning of the baptismal rite: "Three times were you plunged in the water and came forth, signifying Christ's burial for three days."[131]

The biblical symbolism of water, found predominantly in the stories of the Flood and the Red Sea passage, suggests both *death* and *salvation*. So, in Baptism, the Christian is "crucified with Christ" (Galatians 2:19). The old man is put to death and the guilt of his sin, both original and personal sin, dies with him. As the earth was cleansed from sin by the Flood, so we, too, are washed clean in the waters of mercy.[132]

At the same time, through Baptism, the Christian already shares in Christ's resurrection. For this reason, St. Paul says, "You *were buried* with him in baptism, in which you *were also raised* with him" (Colossians 2:12; emphasis added). Jesus is the "first-born from the dead" (Colossians 1:18). In Baptism, we are "born of water and the Spirit" (John 3:5) and become sons and daughters in the Son.

The Israelites' crossing of the Jordan River when they entered Canaan is also a type of Baptism, for Baptism is the entry into the true Promised Land—the kingdom of God. Baptism not only delivers from bondage to the Evil One (as the Israelites had been in bondage to Pharaoh) but also ushers us into our heavenly inheritance.

In the sacrament of Baptism, we receive the Holy Spirit; Baptism is, therefore, the first phase of our participation in Pentecost. We become temples of the Holy Spirit, God-within-us. The Sanctifier, the uncreated Grace, brings with him every good gift: sanctifying grace, the virtues, the gifts, and charisms.

The Lord marks us as his own in Baptism, which is symbolized by the Sign of the Cross made on the forehead of the newly baptized—a custom that goes all the way back to apostolic times and is still part of the baptismal rite today. Made from forehead to heart, left shoulder to right, this sign symbolizes the shield of faith (see Ephesians 6:16). The Sign of the Cross is a shorthand form of the entire creed, reminding us of the Cross, the very center of the creed, and the three divine Persons named in each of the creed's three stanzas. Every time we make this sign, we are renewing our baptismal vows, our personal commitment to Jesus Christ as Lord and Savior, and proclaiming our trust in what he did for us on the Cross.

Confirmation

While the Spirit is given in Baptism (see Acts 2:38), the sacrament of Confirmation bequeaths a fuller outpouring of the Spirit and represents a completion of the baptismal grace.[133] It is, in a sense, the second phase of our sharing in the miracle of Pentecost.

The early Church saw the Spirit's descent upon Jesus *after* his baptism as pointing to Confirmation (see Matthew 3:16)—the sacrament whereby we are "anointed" with the Spirit and become Christians in the full sense (see Acts 10:38).[134]

While Baptism incorporates us into Christ's death and resurrection, Confirmation makes us share in Christ's anointing—his mission as priest, prophet, and king. The sacred chrism consecrates and commits us to a life of worship (i.e., a share in Christ's *priesthood*), evangelization (Christ's *prophetic* witness), and service (Christ's *kingly* service). Israelite kings of old, like David, battled Israel's enemies; Christ's kingly service—as well as our share in it—includes spiritual warfare against the ultimate enemy (see Ephesians 5:10–17). In this sense, Confirmation makes us soldiers of Christ who share the battlefield with him.

Confirmation also more perfectly unites us with the apostolic foundation of the Church—that is, with the apostles and their successors. In the Western tradition, the bishop, as successor of the Apostles, is the ordinary minister of this sacrament.[135] In the East, the ordinary minister is the priest. In both cases, however, the sacred chrism used for the anointing of Confirmation can only be consecrated by the bishop. So, whenever a person is confirmed, in the East or West, he or she is essentially being consecrated by a successor of the apostles to share in the Church's apostolic mission.

The Eucharist

Since the Eucharist is "sacrament of sacraments"—the chief and greatest sacrament—we will devote the entire next chapter to it.

Here, let us say that the Eucharist is the final sacrament of initiation, where a Christian is fully incorporated into the Church, the Body of Christ. This is unclear to many since, for the past 100 years or so, most Catholics in the Western Church who were baptized as infants have received the Eucharist around age seven and Confirmation a few years later. The traditional order, however, was for the Eucharist to be received as the final and climactic entrance into the life of grace.[136]

Unlike Baptism and Confirmation, this sacrament is not received just once. Rather, as food for the journey, it is the new manna that sustains us as we journey to the ultimate Promised Land—heaven itself. Just as the manna fell daily, so, too, is the Eucharist offered to us every day.

Reconciliation

The sacrament of Reconciliation goes by several different names, each highlighting a distinct aspect of the sacrament. "Reconciliation" points to what this sacrament accomplishes; it reconciles us to God and his family, the Church. "Confession" points to the essential act of disclosing our sins to God and his appointed mediator. And "penance" points to our need for not just forgiveness but healing and restoration even after we have been forgiven.

Baptism is the original sacrament of forgiveness. It washes away all sin, but it does not remove all the effects of sin (see CCC 405). We retain, for example, our inclination to sin, and we continue to be tempted by the cares of the world, the weakness of the flesh, and the assaults of the devil (see Mark 4:15–17). So how do we deal with the sins we commit after Baptism, especially the mortal sins? We go to confession. Reconciliation is the sacrament of God's ongoing mercy and our call to continuous, ever-deeper conversion. As Pope St. John Paul II liked to say, here in this sacrament a person faces the gap between the *person-I-am* and the *person-I-am-called-to-be*.

All the sacraments are efficacious because it is Jesus who performs them. So, too, in Reconciliation: It is *Jesus who forgives our sin through the priest*. Here, Christ comes to meet us with compassion as we struggle with our brokenness. It is a gift for us to hear audibly, "Your sins are forgiven." We do not have to rely on our own feelings about being forgiven; rather, we *know* we are forgiven because we trust the objective power of the sacrament.

In Reconciliation, Jesus pours out the grace of the Spirit to heal us and help us repair the harm we have done both to ourselves and to others. We cooperate with this gift by doing the penance assigned by the confessor.

Penances are not done to earn God's forgiveness. No, forgiveness comes to us as a free gift. The work of penance is like a form of therapy and reparation. It is done to heal us and restore wholeness. We make "amends" in this way to cooperate with God's saving work, for he wills not only our forgiveness but also our healing and transformation. The latter is not completely brought about by the declaration of our forgiveness—for our sins (even after we have been forgiven) still leave their marks and wounds upon us. Through God's power (and our cooperation), he wills to remove the last vestiges of the residue of sin from our lives, a work that he begins here—and, if need be, completes in purgatory.

Any remaining vestige of sin hinders our joy and full communion with God. The reason we do penance (and the reason for purgatory) is because God loves us so much that he wants us to *fully* share in Christ's victory over sin—a victory that brings about not just our forgiveness but also our definitive healing and transformation.

Anointing of the Sick

Jesus healed the man born blind by anointing his eyes (see John 9:6–7), and his disciples "anointed with oil many that were sick and healed them" (Mark 6:13). This anointing by the apostles prefigures the sacrament of the Anointing of the Sick, which finds further expression in the early Church (see James 5:13–17).[137]

This sacrament is ordered to the healing of body and soul, received when a person is in danger of death. For this reason, it is also closely tied to the mystery of redemptive suffering—the way in which our suffering, united to Jesus' suffering on the Cross, mysteriously participates in Christ's work of redemption (see Colossians 1:24). As contemporary spiritual writer Jacques Philippe put it, "In all people who suffer there is Jesus who suffers."[138] In this way, the meaning of our suffering is never lost, which gives us a never-failing reason for hope. Only in heaven will we see the true fruits of the suffering we have offered up in union with Jesus.

At the end of life, this sacrament is joined with the sacraments of Reconciliation and the Eucharist as a way of summing up the final stage of our journey. Received at the end of life, the Eucharist is referred to as *viaticum*, food "for the journey" as we "pass over" from death into life. This sacramental triad at the end of life (anointing, confession, and viaticum) parallels the three sacraments of initiation that began our Christian journey.[139]

Holy Orders

Jesus is the one priest; all priesthood is a participation in *his* priesthood (see CCC 662). When he explicitly empowers the apostles through the Holy Spirit to continue the ministry of forgiveness of sins (see John 20:20–23), and when he commands them to "do this in remembrance of me" at the Last Supper (Luke 22:19), Jesus empowers them to continue his work. Jesus continues his priesthood through the apostles and their successors.

St. Paul speaks of the "gift" that was given to Timothy through the laying on of hands (see 1 Timothy 4:14). This refers to power given through the Spirit in sacramental ordination, enabling the minister to continue Jesus' priestly ministry through the sacraments.

Jesus has not left us. In fact, his presence now is in a real way superior to when he walked the earth before his death: in the sacraments, Jesus is present to us at *all times* and *all places*—whereas in his earthly ministry, before his passion and death, if he was in one place, he was not in another. This is why Christ says, "It is to your advantage that I go away" (John 16:7): because, when he returns to the Father, he and the Father send the Spirit, who makes possible Christ's ongoing presence among us, most especially through the sacraments.

Through the laying on of hands, the apostles transmitted the fullness of the sacrament of Holy Orders to the men we call bishops. Bishops are thus the direct successors to the apostles. In fact, the election of St. Matthias was the Church's first episcopal ordination (see Acts 1:12–26).[140] Other men were chosen by the apostles and ordained as "presbyters" (see Acts 14:23), or what we now call "priests." Still others, like Sts. Stephen and Philip, were ordained deacons (See Acts 6:1–7).

Matrimony

Marriage exists throughout the biblical narrative. As the Bible opens with the marriage of Adam and Eve (see Genesis 2), it closes with the "marriage supper of the Lamb" (Revelation 19:9).

Like all the sacraments, marriage is a visible reality that makes present an unseen mystery—namely, Christ's love for his bride, the Church. What

Christ calls us to here is literally *not possible by human power alone*. We are called to love in a supernatural way; in marriage, spouses are to love one another "as Christ loved the church and gave himself up for her" (Ephesians 5:25). This is why the vows recited at the altar by the bride and groom conclude with the words "as long as we both shall live." Marital love is both a life-giving union and a love unto death. It is an indissoluble union, one that cannot be severed any more than Christ can separate himself from his bride, the Church (see Matthew 19:3–12).

The Old Testament describes God's people as his bride. When Israel is unfaithful, the prophets accuse her of committing *adultery* against her divine spouse (see Ezekiel 16:8–13, 15, 20–21). But the prophets also envision a restoration of this marital union with the Lord (see Hosea 2:14, 16; Isaiah 54:5), which is ultimately fulfilled in Christ.[141] The sacrament of Matrimony makes this spousal union between God and his people manifest in a visible way by empowering couples to love as he does; here—as with all the sacraments—God's invisible love takes visible expression.

Perhaps the most important truth we can grasp about marriage, then, is that it points beyond itself. As a sacrament, marriage makes present a love that goes beyond our wildest imaginations—God's unconditional love for us. That is why the sacrament exists—to give us the grace to love in a truly *supernatural* way, to love as God loves.

Married couples need to draw from this wellspring of grace; this is the only way God's plan for married life can be lived out because it is literally beyond our power to do so. This is precisely why it is a sacrament.

There is great power when couples truly believe in this sacrament. I (Andrew) remember struggles early on in marriage, when my wife and I looked at each other and one of us said, "Well, I'm not going anywhere, and I know you aren't either, so let's fix this problem." There is great *freedom* and *liberating power* in the truth of marital indissolubility.

Easy? Of course not. But tremendously liberating when one embraces the truth of marriage and taps into this powerful grace? *Absolutely*, without question.

The Sacraments: Sharing in Christ's Risen Life

Ancient Jews often thought in terms of two ages: this age and the age to come. Many believed that the age to come would include a general resurrection of all the just at the end of time. What they did not expect was a resurrection of the messiah *in the midst of time.*[142]

What is new for the Christian is to have one foot in the old age—with the vestiges of sin, suffering, and death still present—and one foot already *now* in the age to come. For the resurrection of Jesus has already inaugurated the new age: "If any one is in Christ, he is a *new creation*" (2 Corinthians 5:17; emphasis added). And the sacraments are the means by which we enter into Christ—the means by which we enter the age to come, beginning with Baptism (see Romans 6:3–4).

The sacraments are encounters with the Risen Jesus and an entrance into the paschal mystery of his life, death, resurrection, and ascension, enabling us to share in his divinity (see 1 Peter 1:3–4). For the mystery of salvation is this: The eternal Son took on our humanity in order to infuse it with his divinity.

The Sacraments: The Mighty Works of God

Have you ever thought of the sacraments as divine *miracles* on a par with God's actions at the Red Sea or Jesus' healing the blind?

This is how the earliest Christians understood the power of the sacraments. In his definitive study of the relationship between the Bible and the sacraments in the first centuries of the Church, Jean Daniélou had this to say:

> The life of ancient Christianity was centered around worship. ... The sacraments were thought of as the essential events of Christian existence, and of existence itself, *as being the prolongation of the great works of God in the Old Testament and the New.* In them was inaugurated a new creation which introduced the Christian even now into the Kingdom of God.[143]

Catholic tradition draws a distinction between the Old Covenant "sacraments" (or signs and rituals, such as circumcision and the ritual sacrifices) and the New Covenant sacraments (i.e., Baptism, etc.). The contrast looks like this:

Old Covenant Signs/Sacraments	New Covenant Sacraments
Many	Few
Burdensome	Easy
Not efficacious	Efficacious

The third item here is key: the signs (or "sacraments") of the Old Covenant were merely *signs* of grace, forgiveness, etc.—that is, they could symbolize these realities but could not truly offer the spiritual grace they signified. What is new in the New Covenant—*the difference that Christ makes*—is that the New Covenant sacraments *truly offer the grace they signify.* That is, the Holy Spirit does what the perceptible signs (e.g., water, oil) signify.

For example, Baptism not only symbolizes spiritual cleansing; the Holy Spirit accomplishes what the water signifies.[144] The visible sign manifests an invisible miracle taking place—a miracle even greater than raising Lazarus from the dead. For Jesus restored Lazarus's body to natural life; the sacraments infuse us with supernatural life—divine life.

CHAPTER 12

The Eucharist: Sacrament of Sacraments

At the Last Supper, Jesus said, "Do this in remembrance of me" (Luke 22:19). While most Christians have a communion service of some kind, many Christian communities view it simply as a reminder of what Jesus did for us on Calvary in the distant past.

But, from the very beginning until the sixteenth century, virtually all Christians believed something quite different about the memorial Jesus instituted on the night before he died. They believed (as Catholics have always believed) that Christ is truly present in the Eucharist—Body and Blood, Soul and Divinity—under the appearance of the bread and the wine.

Everything in Catholic life revolves around this rich yet mysterious celebration. St. Irenaeus, writing around AD 180, describes the centrality of the Eucharist this way: "Our way of thinking is attuned to the Eucharist, and the Eucharist in turn confirms our way of thinking."[145]

In all the sacraments, Jesus, the Divine Word of God, is present and active, communicating his transforming grace through the power of the Holy Spirit. But, in this sacrament, not only does he give us his grace in a unique way, he gives us *himself*—so completely that it is the most intimate and complete encounter with him possible this side of heaven.

Exodus and Passover Fulfilled

We can best appreciate the Church's teaching on the Eucharist by recovering the biblical perspective of ancient Israel. We have seen how the Exodus provides the template of God's saving work in Christ: bondage to Pharaoh is an image of our bondage to sin and Satan; deliverance through water foreshadows Baptism and entrance into the kingdom; and the saving blood of the Passover Lamb and the miracle of the manna point ahead to the Eucharist.

The Jewish Passover feast became a yearly memorial (see Exodus 12:14) of God's saving act in the Exodus. For the ancient Jews, this memorial of the Passover was not simply a matter of remembering the past. Rather, it meant *entering now into* a saving event that took place in the past. It meant making that past salvation mystically present so that all generations could share in it.

The Mishnah, the most authoritative book for Jews after the Scriptures, expresses this sense of memorial powerfully in relation to Passover: "In every generation a person is duty-bound to regard himself as if he personally has come forth from Egypt."[146] To eat the Passover meal, then, is to be mysteriously shielded from the angel of death and to escape slavery as if, through this liturgical memorial, one were coming forth from Egypt in the present.

This deeply Jewish notion of memorial as *making present* lies behind Jesus' words at the Last Supper: "Do this in *remembrance* of me" (Luke 22:19; 1 Corinthians 11:25; emphasis added). Jesus is commanding the apostles to repeat his actions as a liturgical memorial—and so make the paschal mystery present so that every future generation can share in Jesus' saving work.

Importantly, in the original Passover, it was never enough just to slay the lamb; the sacrifice was not complete until the lamb was consumed (see Exodus 12:8). In this, we can see an intimate bond between the Last Supper, the Cross, and the Eucharist. Jesus begins his sacrifice at the Last Supper—and what he begins there culminates on the Cross. But the sacrifice is not complete until the lamb is consumed. That is why, after St. Paul refers to Jesus as the Passover Lamb, he insists that we still need to keep the feast (see 1 Corinthians 5:7–8)—because consuming the Risen Lamb in the Holy Eucharist is essential to our sharing in this new Passover.

The memorial of the Eucharist makes present the entire movement of the Last Supper, the Cross, and Jesus' resurrection.

While the English word "Easter" does not make this obvious, Easter celebrates the New Covenant Passover—the deliverance of mankind not merely from Egypt but from sin and death. In English, we hear this when we speak of the paschal mystery (drawn from the Greek word *pascha,* which means "Passover"). In Italian, we hear it in the Easter greeting *Buona Pasqua*.[147]

Jesus' Sacrifice Transcends Time

The teaching of the Catholic Church is unambiguous: There is no other saving sacrifice except the one that Jesus offered on Calvary (see Hebrews 10:12). That sacrifice cannot be repeated. And, since it is forever sufficient, there is no need to supplement it. The Eucharist, therefore, neither repeats it nor adds to it; rather, it is a re-presentation (*memorial*) of that sacrifice—it makes this one sacrifice present.

The sacrifice that Jesus offered once and for all was a unique act. He was a real man, so it was an act that took place at a particular time and place in the past. But Jesus is also true God, who is outside time and lives in the eternal present: Past and future are always present to him. This means that the actions of Christ on Calvary and on Easter Sunday morning are not only human acts taking place in history but also eternal, divine acts that can be made present in all times and places by the power of the Spirit.

This is what happens in the Eucharist. The power of the Cross—the atoning sacrifice that forgives, liberates, heals, and reconciles—becomes present and available, allowing us to enter this great mystery.

As wonderful as this is, the Cross is incomplete without the Resurrection (see Romans 4:25). The entire paschal mystery—Jesus' exodus from this world into glory—is a single saving event, and the Eucharist is its memorial. This means that the Resurrection, too, is made present every time the Eucharist is celebrated. When we go to Mass, we are at the foot of the

Cross, watching the Savior give his life for us. Yet we are also outside the empty tomb with the risen Jesus and the women who greeted him on that wonderful morning.

Eucharist, Sunday, and the Resurrection

Sunday is really a weekly memorial of Easter. For that reason, is it the pre-eminent eucharistic day. This is explicitly expressed in the following prayer recited at each Sunday Eucharist in the Maronite Catholic Church of Antioch:

> When we ponder, O Christ, the marvels accomplished on this day, the Sunday of your holy resurrection, we say: "Blessed is Sunday, for on it began creation ... the world's salvation ... the renewal of the human race. ... On Sunday heaven and earth rejoiced and the whole universe was filled with light. Blessed is Sunday, for on it were opened the gates of paradise so that Adam and all the exiles might enter it without fear."
>
> —Quoted in CCC 1167

Because of the Resurrection, Sunday becomes the first day of the new creation. In this way, the Sabbath of the old creation (seventh day) gives way to the Sunday of the new creation (see Acts 20:7). Early Christians often referred to Sunday as the "eighth day"—the first and the last, the eternal day of the new creation.[148]

His Sacrifice Expanded in Us

In a real way, the Eucharist is also *our* sacrifice too (see 1 Peter 2:5). As members of his body, we join our own offerings to the offering of our divine head. How do we do this? First, we offer a sacrifice of praise and thanksgiving (which is the literal meaning of the word Eucharist).[149] We join our prayers to those of the priest when, in the Eucharistic Prayer, in the name of us all, he thanks the Father for the splendid goodness of his creation, for the entire history of salvation, and for its culmination in the incarnation, death, resurrection, and ascension of Jesus.

If you are not in the habit of silently adding your own personalized thanksgiving to the Eucharistic Prayer said by the priest, try it next time you are at Mass. Thank God for his many gifts, both in salvation history and especially for his work in our lives personally.

But our Eucharistic sacrifice involves more than offering praise and thanksgiving for what God has done. It means, second, offering *ourselves* to him in response, as St. Paul describes: "I appeal to you therefore, brethren, by the mercies of God, to present your bodies as a living sacrifice, holy and acceptable to God, which is your spiritual worship" (Romans 12:1).

As the gifts are brought forward in Mass, we should consciously put ourselves and everything in our lives on the altar—our time, ambitions, possessions, relationships, work, and trials. For the Eucharist is indeed "an altar call." With the gifts, we should consciously place our hearts on the altar as well.

In this way, the Mass becomes the offering of the entire body of Christ, head and members, as we fully enter into the paschal mystery of Christ—his death and resurrection.

The privilege of sharing in Jesus' perfect sacrifice is symbolized beautifully just before the consecration, when the priest mixes a few drops of water with the wine. The paltry sacrifice of our lives is like the water that is absorbed into the rich sacrifice of Christ, symbolized by the wine.

But nothing is small in God's eyes. From the vantage point of eternity, our seemingly small offerings here in Christ can move mountains. Our entire lives, struggles, and triumphs become eminently more meaningful in Christ—far more than we could ever imagine!

The Personal Presence of Christ

Christ is present to us in the Mass in many ways. The Church recognizes four in particular: in the congregation, in the person of the priest, in the Liturgy of the Word, and in the Eucharistic species.[150]

In the Congregation

First, Christ is present in his body—the Church. Jesus said he is present whenever two or more people are gathered in his name (see Matthew 18:20). Those filing into a church for Mass are not just a collection of random individuals but members of Christ's body. Whether conscious of it or not, they are being drawn and built together by the Holy Spirit into the body of Christ.

What we do or do not do to the least of them, we do or do not do to Christ (see Matthew 25:40, 45). We do not approach him as individuals but together, as the body of Christ. We dare not approach his altar unless we are at peace with one another, which is the meaning of the Sign of Peace (see Matthew 5:23–4).[151]

In the Person of the Priest

Second, Christ is present at Mass in the person of the priest. Christ's presence does not depend on the priest's personal virtue. Christ makes himself present through the anointing given to the priest in the sacrament of Holy Orders. The liturgical vestments worn by the priest remind us that the priest is acting in the Person of Christ, not in his own person. The ordained priest is an icon and instrument of Christ, the true priest. Through him, Jesus makes his priesthood present.[152] Hence, at the consecration, the priest does not say, "This is *his* Body," but "This is *my* Body."

In the Liturgy of the Word

Third, Jesus is present in the Eucharist in the Word of God.

The Catholic Church's respect for the value and power of the inspired Word of God is reflected in every sacramental celebration, especially in the Eucharist. The first half of the Liturgy of the Mass revolves around Sacred Scripture.

It is not just at the table of the altar that we are nourished. The ambo, where the Gospel is read, is also like a table, as the Second Vatican Council explains: "The Church has always venerated the divine Scriptures just as she venerates the Body of the Lord, since from the table of both the Word of God and of the Body of Christ she unceasingly receives and offers to the faithful the Bread of Life, especially in the Sacred Liturgy."[153] We read the Scriptures first because they build up our faith. Christ is present in them, preparing us to discern the real presence of his Body and Blood under the signs of bread and wine.

In addition to the readings, the living Word of God comes to us through the prayers of Mass. Listen carefully, and you will discover that these prayers are almost entirely scriptural. For example, the *Gloria* is taken from the shepherds in Luke 2; the *Kyrie* ("Lord have mercy") is drawn from the prayer of the tax collector in Luke 18:13 and the pleas of various lepers to Jesus (see Luke 17:13). And, before receiving the Eucharist, we pray the words of the centurion who says he is not worthy to have Jesus come under his roof (see Matthew 8:8), for, as Pope St. John Paul II once said, we need the humility of the centurion before we approach the Bread of Life (see *Ecclesia de Eucharistia,* 48).

Additionally, the Alleluia, the Lamb of God, the Hosanna, the Holy, Holy, Holy—all come directly from Scripture. The Liturgy's use of Scripture here helps us place ourselves in the great biblical story, making its words our very own.[154]

In the Bread and Wine, His Body and Blood

The final and most sublime way that the Lord is present in the Mass is in his Body and Blood, present to us under the signs of bread and wine.

Jesus is God, and God is everywhere. But Jesus is now and forever man as well as God; his humanity cannot be present everywhere in the same way as his divinity. Jesus' glorified humanity is in heaven at the Father's right hand. In the Eucharist and only in the Eucharist, he makes his entire being, his humanity and divinity—Body and Blood, Soul and Divinity—present to us truly and really. This is why the sacramental presence of Christ's Body and Blood is so extraordinary. In all the other sacraments, Jesus gives us his divine grace, but in the Eucharist, the sacrament of sacraments, he gives us his entire self, divinity and humanity.[155]

How can Jesus be present bodily under the forms of bread and wine? The transformation of food and drink into Christ's Body and Blood happens the same way Mary's virginal conception did: through the power of the Word and the Spirit. It happens the same way creation did: the world was made out of nothing through the power of the Word and the Spirit (see Genesis 1:1–3). Likewise, in the Eucharist, the One who said, "Let there be light," also says, "This is my Body," and, "This is my Blood." At the same time that he speaks his Word, he sends down his Spirit. And the awesome change takes place. God's word is efficacious; he accomplishes what he declares, and he does so in the very act of his declaring it.

About the year 1200, as some theologians were struggling to find a way to explain this marvelous change, they came up with the word *transubstantiation*.[156] One reason some people struggle with this term is that the word "substance" can mean different things. For us, substance is something you can touch. Substance abuse has to do with chemicals like drugs and alcohol. In theology, though, *substance* means something that *underlies* what you can see and touch; it is the essence of the thing that "stands under" (*sub-stantia*) its appearances. Surface characteristics—what theologians call "accidents"—describe the qualities of a thing that are perceptible to the senses (i.e., the appearances).

Transubstantiation, therefore, means that while everything looks the same on the surface (the appearances do not change), the underlying essence of the thing is totally transformed. This is just the opposite of what happens in everyday experience. Usually, appearances change while the essence of a thing stays the same. For example, if I get a suntan, I am still the same person. But in the Eucharist, the underlying, invisible substance is transformed even though the appearances remain the same. The substance of bread and wine becomes Christ's Body and Blood. Under a microscope, you would not be able to tell the difference, for the level at which this change happens is far too deep for human probing because it is not perceptible with the senses.[157] In the Eucharist, Christ is as truly present in his Body and Blood, Soul and Divinity, as when he walked the roads of Galilee.

Analogously, if one performed open-heart surgery upon Jesus back in Galilee, his internal anatomy would not have revealed his true identity as the divine Son of God. So also with the Eucharist: Appearances do not reveal the full truth. Jesus is God in the flesh—both in Galilee and in his Eucharistic species.

When he comes again at the end of time, he will not have any more glory than he does right now in the Blessed Sacrament; the only difference will be in our ability to see.

A Banquet Like No Other

The Eucharist is a meal. It is the Lord's Supper as well as a holy sacrifice. It has to be both. Christ becomes present so that we can not only see him under the signs or appearances of bread and wine but also consume him as our food.

But why bread and wine?

In John 6, Jesus says, "I am the bread of life" (v. 35), presenting himself as the bread "which comes down from heaven, and gives life to the world" (v. 33). His words link his body, later given in the Eucharist, with the manna that God rained down from heaven to sustain the people of Israel on their journey to the Promised Land.

Wine is the blood of the grape. To obtain it, the fruit must be crushed. Wine, therefore, symbolizes the cup of suffering, recalling the price Jesus paid to save us and do the Father's will.

Wine also symbolizes the cup of joy. In both Old Testament and New Testament times, wine was associated with festivity. Wine "cheers gods and men" (Judges 9:13) and serves to "gladden the heart of man" (Psalm 104:15). The wedding feast of Cana is a prime example of wine symbolizing the overflowing joy of the messianic age (see John 2). So wine both points back to Jesus' death on the Cross and points forward to the messianic banquet—the wedding feast of the risen Lamb (see Revelation 19:9).

The symbol of wine—the blood of the grape that becomes the Blood of Jesus—is even richer if we understand the significance of blood in the Old Testament. There, blood is equated with life, which is why the Mosaic Law forbade consuming the blood of animals (see Leviticus 17:14). Even though mankind was created on the sixth day with the other animals, we are not to share their *life*.

Jesus speaks to this understanding of blood and life when he says, "Truly, truly, I say to you, unless you eat the flesh of the Son of man and *drink his blood, you have no life in you*" (John 6:53; emphasis added). In effect, Jesus is saying, "While you are not to share the life of animals, *you are to share life of the God-man.*"

In the Eucharist, Jesus gives us a share in God's divine life by giving us his own Blood so that we might share in his divine nature (see 2 Peter 1:4). What is this divine nature? Essentially, it is the inner life of the Trinity: three Persons eternally pouring themselves out in self-giving love for one another. This is *agape,* or charity (see 1 John 4:8). Drinking the precious Blood of the risen Jesus gives us an opportunity to have Christ's sacred heart beating in our breasts and the divine life of charity coursing through our veins.

The One we take upon our lips and into our bodies in the Eucharist is the same Jesus who raised Lazarus and healed the man born blind. In Holy Communion we receive Jesus, the risen Lord who will come again in glory to judge the living and the dead.

And, in receiving our Risen Lord in the Eucharist, we have hope in our own resurrection on the last day. In St. Ignatius of Antioch's words, writing around AD 107, the Eucharist is the "medicine of immortality, antidote against death" (*Letter to the Ephesians,* ch. 20).

Bearing Fruit

The same night that he instituted the Eucharist, Jesus told us that he is the vine and we are the branches. Our role is to bear much fruit (see John 15). God's design for all the sacraments, and especially the Eucharist, is that they bear fruit in everyone who partakes of them and in the Church as a whole. As the saying goes, "You are what you eat." The Father gives us the bread of life, the Body of Christ, to make us more of what we are— corporately the Church, the body of Christ, and individually fruitful and holy members of that body.[158]

Obviously, none of us still this side of heaven are yet perfectly sanctified. And many who attend Mass and even receive Communion seem to be making little progress. "You will know them by their fruits" (Matthew 7:20).

How does this fact line up with the teaching of the Church on the Eucharist?

In the Eucharist, the Lord is faithful to his promise to be present and make his life-changing grace available (see Matthew 28:20). The Church teaches that the objective reality of the sacraments has nothing to do with the faith or lack of faith of either the minister or the people.[159] Grace is made available by the sovereign act of Christ.

But the fruit that is born in those who receive the sacrament has everything to do with their dispositions. Unrepentant sin renders the grace of the sacraments ineffective. So does unforgiveness and resentment. Lack of faith likewise limits its intended fruit.[160]

Recall the story of the woman who touched Jesus as he made his way through the crowded streets of an unnamed town in Galilee. Many people surrounded him, and some even physically bumped into him. But of those who touched him, only she was healed. She had reached out to him in expectant faith and touched the hem of his garment. Jesus knew immediately that power had flowed out of him, and he turned to discover her at his feet, trembling. Instantly, the hemorrhaging that had plagued her for many years stopped (see Luke 8:40–48).

Like her faith, our faith is the ground in which the grace of the Eucharist grows and bears fruit, or else withers and dies.

The grace of the Eucharist is always objectively on offer, but will we approach in faith and truly avail ourselves of this most august treasure in our midst?

The Eucharist as the Messianic Banquet

The covenant at Sinai begins with the proclamation of God's Word, the Ten Commandments, followed by a solemn sacrifice. And it proceeds to a sacred *communion meal* in the very presence of God. Moses, Aaron, Nadab, Abihu, and seventy elders go up to the top of Mt. Sinai into God's very presence. They see the God of Israel and enjoy a banquet meal as the culmination of the covenant ceremony. Going from *word* to *sacrifice* and now to sacred banquet *meal*, "they beheld God, and ate and drank" (Exodus 24:11).

This sacred meal atop Mt. Sinai became the prototype of what God will do in the messianic age—bringing about a new Exodus that culminates in a sacred banquet meal in the very presence of God.[161]

Isaiah in particular gives poignant expression to this hope when he foretells a future "feast" marked by "choice wines" (Isaiah 25:6)—a feast which is for "all peoples" (v. 6). And through this feast, the Lord will "swallow up death forever" and "the reproach of his people he will take away from all the earth" (v. 8).[162] In other words, through this meal, death and sin will be overcome.

Thus, for Isaiah, the future messianic age is said to be inaugurated by:

- a liturgical "feast,"
- marked by rich "wine,"
- which overcomes death,
- and definitively deals with sin.

Intriguingly, this same section of Isaiah also speaks of *resurrection*: "Your dead shall live, their bodies shall rise. O dwellers in the dust, awake and sing for joy!" (Isaiah 26:19).[163]

At the Last Supper, the apostles witness the fulfillment of Isaiah's hope: At the dawn of the Messianic age, they share a banquet meal—in the very presence of God, the God-man, Jesus Christ. This meal is marked by rich wine, the "chalice of his blood," and is offered ultimately for all people—a meal that sets in motion the Lord's defeat of sin and death forever.

This messianic banquet is indeed the "marriage supper of the lamb" (Revelation 19:9) already anticipated in the Last Supper. It is the fulfillment of what was foreshadowed on Mt. Sinai in Exodus 24 and prophesied by Isaiah: the liturgical banquet meal in the very presence of God that inaugurates the Messianic age to come and overcomes the power of sin and death.

Manna and the Eucharist

The Exodus serves as the primary backdrop for the paschal mystery of Christ made present in our midst through the sacraments of the New Covenant. The water from the rock (see Exodus 17:6), for example, points to Baptism and the gift of the Spirit (see 1 Corinthians 10:1–5).

The manna, likewise, is food for the journey *after* the Exodus and *before* one gets to the Promised Land. That is, the manna *ceases* when Israel arrives at the Promised Land (see Joshua 5:12). In fact, the "taste" of the manna is said to be like "honey" (Exodus 16:31), reminiscent of the description of the hoped-for Promised Land as a land flowing with "milk and *honey*" (Exodus 3:8; emphasis added). Hence, the manna is truly a foretaste of the Promised Land, which ceases when they arrive at the real thing!

In a similar way, the Eucharist is a *foretaste of heaven*. And while the Eucharist already *is* the reality—it *is* Jesus risen among us—in heaven the sign of the Eucharist will give way to face to face communion, just as the manna ceased when they arrived at the Promised Land.

For it is the plan of the Son of God to make us and the whole Church partake in his mysteries and to extend them to and continue them in us and in his whole Church. This is his plan for fulfilling his mysteries in us.

— *St. John Eudes*

CHAPTER 13

Catholic Spirituality and the Call to Holiness

Some look at religion, especially Christianity, as a crutch for weak people. It is designed, they think, to make people subservient, passive weaklings who never spread their wings and realize their natural potential.

The irony is that this is, in fact, exactly what sin does. Despite its empty promises of excitement and fulfillment, sin isolates, wounds, and debilitates us, enslaving us to the world, the flesh, and the devil. We have already seen this in examining the story of Adam and Eve (see Genesis 2–3).

God created us in his image and likeness, which means we were created to be vibrantly alive and gloriously free. Jesus said, "If the Son makes you free, you will be free indeed" (John 8:36). Elsewhere, he exclaimed, "I came that they may have life, and have it abundantly" (John 10:10). God's whole program of redemption, therefore, includes more than merely acquitting us of our sin. He wants to go on to liberate us, strengthen us, and restore our dignity. This progressive rehabilitation process begins with the moment of our Baptism and continues until it finds its final fulfillment in heavenly glory. This lifelong movement of continual conversion is called sanctification or divinization (*theosis*). The primary agent in this process is Christ working through his Holy Spirit, the Sanctifier.

But if we were merely passive objects in this process of transformation, it would do little to restore our dignity. As persons, we are not *objects* but *subjects.* As persons, we need to actively participate in our own healing, growth, and liberation. God has such tremendous respect for our freedom that he will do nothing in us without our consent and cooperation.

We have seen already that faith is all about *walking*, not sitting still. The woman with the flow of blood took the initiative to reach out and touch Jesus (see Luke 8:43–48). There is no way to become stronger except through exercise.

Training Champions

The call to holiness is the call to arise and become champions. In athletics, no champions are simply born. They must be made. Life is a pure gift, for sure. But people who are entrusted with great gifts vary in what they do with them. Many who receive the gift of arms and legs exercise them only enough to walk to the refrigerator and open the door. Others train and develop to such an extent that they win Olympic medals.

St. Paul often explains the spiritual life in athletic terms. "Train yourself in godliness; for while bodily training is of some value, godliness is of value in every way, as it holds promise for the present life and also for the life to come. ... For to this end we toil and strive" (1 Timothy 4:7–8, 10).[164] This sounds a little arduous. But it is hard to argue with Paul's logic. Intense exercise leads to gains in strength, flexibility, stamina, and energy. It is well worth the effort just on the natural and physical level; how much more so when the training regimen yields eternal benefits.

To be physically fit all the way around, a person needs to engage in three different sorts of disciplines: diet, strength training, and cardio. You must control what goes into your mouth, work on muscle strength, and not neglect the most important muscle of all: the heart. There are, though, many different forms of diet, strength training, and cardio. You and your trainer pick the best combo to suit you as you begin your program and carry it out. If you are a serious athlete, the training may change over time, but it never ends.

True Catholic conversion is always ongoing. Even if there is a clear "before" and "after" moment in terms of when we gave our lives to the Lord, conversion is never merely a one-time moment; it continues for a lifetime.

The Danger of Being Our Own "Boss"

Both in fitness and in sports training, there is real danger in being our own boss. This is even more true in the spiritual and moral life.

It is probably not hard for each of us to think of a time when we really wanted to do something we knew we shouldn't. At such moments, we have two options: We can realign our passions with right reason. Or, as happens more often than not, we can cook up some good "reasons" to justify doing what we want to do. It's called *rationalization*.

As we know all too well, rationalizations easily spiral, and, after a while, we end up in a moral and spiritual place where we never dreamed we would be.

Here is the truth: greatness in anything, including the spiritual life, requires *accountability*.

This is why the Magisterium, the teaching of the authority of the Church, is such a precious gift. For the fact is that authentic love must be grounded in the truth. In moral and spiritual matters, it is very easy to deceive ourselves; it is very easy to latch on only to the "truths" that suit us and avoid what challenges us.

The truths of the Church's doctrine are like the banks of a river that enable the water to rush downstream with power and vitality. Without firm banks, the water—instead of rushing forth—becomes stagnant and lazy, going nowhere. That is what our spiritual and moral lives look like when they lack clear boundaries in objective truth. Without them, many people today suffer from a spiritual and moral "aimlessness" that becomes a source of sadness and lethargy—a spiritual malaise that saps life of its energy, leaving many bored, restless, and unfulfilled.

The Church's Magisterium, guided by the Holy Spirit, illumines our path with doctrines about the Trinity, Jesus, and redemption. But the Church's teaching authority also extends to clarifying the natural moral law and its place in the Christian life. Taking the teaching authority of the Church seriously helps us to not fall into the trap of being our own boss. It helps us avoid the temptation of manufacturing excuses as to why our individual situation is an exception to the rules—an easy thing to tell ourselves, especially when the truth seems to stand in the way of what we want! Real integrity, real spiritual maturity, entails a readiness to conform our wants and desires to objective truth instead of trying to twist the truth to conform to our wishes and desires.

This is never easy. But being our own boss is a recipe for disaster in the spiritual life, for we naturally latch on to truths that comfort us and reject those that challenge us. In the end, our autonomy becomes (unwittingly) the worship of our own egos. And it prevents us from ever fully entering into the transformation that awaits us when we surrender to the truth that is outside us—the truth that we did not create ourselves. The gift of the Magisterium (which we can readily find in the *Catechism*) enables us to know the truth of God's revelation with ease. It is not hard to find out what the Church teaches, to know the truth—but it will always be hard to live it out.

This "challenge" of the Gospel—the challenge of a Gospel with real teeth—is exactly what sparked my (Andrew's) conversion in college; it is, in fact, what finally made the Gospel worthwhile for me. I found that I could only give my life for a Gospel that truly costs something, that truly makes a claim on my life. Only then did I find life truly exhilarating and meaningful—far more so than all my years of football. Here, I finally found the battle I was truly longing for.

What Is Life All About?

For a great many people today, life is a story with no plot. Each of us is supposed to give meaning to our own life—as the saying goes, "You do you"—quintessentially being our own boss. But, deep down, many sense the emptiness here. As Joseph Ratzinger put it, "Meaning that is *self-made* is in the last analysis no meaning." Real meaning cannot be made "but only received."[165]

The classical world of Greek philosophy often discerned a clear goal in life. Life had a goal, we each had a destiny, and the *virtues* were the skills we needed to reach the goal. What became known as the four cardinal virtues (which are also mentioned in the book of Wisdom 8:7)—prudence, justice, courage, and temperance—were thought to be the virtues on which a good life hinged. A "good" man or woman in this context is not simply a "nice guy" but rather one who has attained the *skills* to live life with excellence. Practically speaking, the good man or woman is the one who has attained the skills to fulfill their relationships—to be a good son or daughter, husband or wife, father or mother. Life was not simply about *me* and my self-aggrandizing goals; it was not simply "I do me." It was about fulfilling my *relationships*.

Further, the whole notion of virtue formation was about more than what happened on the outside—more than external acts. Rather, the life of virtue was all about becoming a certain kind of person on the inside.

In any given sport, anybody can hit a lucky shot, but the good player's performance is consistent and reliable. Similarly, a truly virtuous person can perform virtuous actions *consistently, promptly,* and with *joy*—on demand, as it were. This person has the skills to be a good friend, a good father or mother, a good husband or wife—skills that free him or her to live life with excellence.

This is a deeper view of freedom than what we are used to. I (Andrew) often ask the students in my Christian Moral Life class if they are *free* to speak French. Mildly humored, they look at me with a smirk, saying of course they are. At this point, I politely ask them to do so. Then they explain to me that they *could* if they really wanted to, but, since they haven't studied French, they are unable to do so at the moment.

At this point, I explain to them that in that case, *they really aren't free to speak French* after all because they have not yet attained the *skills* that would enable them to do so—certainly not on demand and with joy.

In other words, freedom can be superficially understood as simply the ability to do whatever I want ("You do you"). But the deeper freedom is *the ability to do the good.* This freedom grows with practice and discipline; it is not all-or-nothing. The following examples illustrate this deeper view of freedom:

- Learning a foreign language
- Learning a musical instrument
- Getting in shape
- Mastering any athletic skill that at first feels clumsy and awkward but over time becomes fluid and effortless

These things are difficult at first, but they get easier over time with practice. Developing the virtues is like getting into moral shape. The spiritual muscles are strengthened through exercise. They become an interior part of who we are, shaping us into a certain kind of person. In this sense, who we will be five years from now is *directly* related to what we are doing right now. Our moral practice becomes, if not perfect, more and more *permanent.*

In a real sense, our actions dictate who we are. This is the opposite of what we commonly tell ourselves, that "deep down I'm a good guy, *despite what I did last weekend."* As I joke with my students, that is like saying, "Deep down I'm a good pitcher—*I just never throw strikes."* The fact is that each pitch I throw poorly makes it more likely I will throw poorly the next time. Individual acts become habits over time. In and through each pitch, I am in the process of becoming a certain kind of pitcher.

Therefore, the moral question we should ask ourselves is not simply, *What should I do in this or that situation?* but *Who do I want to be?* For in and through each of my decisions, I am becoming a certain kind of person. I am being changed. In every decision, I am answering the question of who I want to be.

Virtues are the skills we need to live life with excellence, the skills that give us true *freedom*—the freedom to live a fulfilling and authentically happy life. For the virtues *free* us to truly love and in this way free us to fulfill our relationships.

We can see, then, that the Christian tradition embraced the virtue framework of classical Greek philosophy and deepened it with the light of faith because the opposite of true freedom is slavery to sin (see John 8:34).

Consider the three theological virtues of faith, hope, and charity in relation to the four cardinal virtues of prudence, justice, temperance, and courage: Faith enhances natural prudence, enabling us to see the world as God sees it. Charity deepens justice and temperance, placing all things in the context of love of God and neighbor—and enables us to love God *in* our neighbor. And hope strengthens courage, enabling us to see that this life is not the end but is rather our preparation for eternity.

In this way, life in the Spirit builds on, heals, perfects, and elevates natural virtue. The true goal of life sought by the ancient Greeks—illumined by faith—is intimate union with God in this life and the next.[166]

The Importance of Prayer

Prayer is critical in our moral and spiritual walk with the Lord.

A brief story illustrates well just how vital prayer is to our ongoing moral and spiritual journey.

A friend of mine once gave a talk on the moral life at a conference; afterward, a young man came up to challenge him forthrightly. It was clear that this young man did not like the notion of objective moral truth. After a few minutes of the discussion going nowhere, my friend simply suggested to this young man that he spend some time with our Lord in the nearby adoration chapel in order to "bring this argument before him."

The young man actually took him up on it and, later, came back to find my friend. The young man proceeded to acknowledge that the real issue driving their earlier engagement was that he had been sleeping with his girlfriend; his provocative confrontation was really a cover for him to justify his course of action to himself.

Notice: *Only in the quiet of prayer did the truth of his spiritual and moral condition come to light.* Only in prayer was he truly able to avoid the temptation of being his own boss—only in prayer was his self-deception unmasked.

As important as the Mass is—as objectively the highest form of prayer (and as important as other forms of vocal prayer are, such as the Rosary)—quiet *listening* prayer is absolutely vital to the spiritual life. For we know all too well how easily one can go to Mass regularly (and perform many types of "vocal" prayer) and yet still live a double life.

It has been rightly said that one cannot persist in this type of quiet listening prayer *and* serious sin: either one will stop praying or stop sinning—but it is very difficult to do both for long.

The reason? This kind of silence with our Lord is just too loud. In the silence, the echo of our Lord's voice resounds, leading over time to the gradual disentangling of our self-deceptions.

This listening prayer can take many forms (adoration, prayerful reading of Scripture, etc.). But what is essential is that we open our minds and hearts and sincerely *listen* to the voice of the Lord; we ask him *what in our life needs to change* and *how we can grow*. As we do this consistently, we will grow in our peace and confidence that we are truly moving in step with the Holy Spirit and his plan for our life.

When we neglect this type of prayer, on the one hand, it becomes all too easy to deceive ourselves (as with the young man above); on the other hand, neglecting this type of prayer often leads to an uneasiness as we navigate life—for deep down we know that *we* are the main ones directing our life and that we have not really given over the entire reins to the Lord.

The Witness of the Saints

In this journey, the saints (as well as living mentors) become our models.[167] It is often very helpful to discover not only their heroism but also how they struggled. For example, I (Andrew) will never forget the first time I came across the great St. Augustine's prayerful quip: "Lord, give me chastity ... *but not yet.*"[168] Coming to know that the great St. Augustine struggled in this way gives hope to those with similar struggles; knowing that a saint struggled and overcame gives us hope that we, too, can overcome as well.

To be Catholic is to take this journey as a family, to do this with one another. Our moral and spiritual journey is never simply truly solitary—it is never just about "me and Jesus." The Church is the Family of God. She teaches us as a mother who loves us enough to speak the hard truths. But she also embraces us with tender mercy. The Church here includes not just our local parish but all those connected to the vine, all those connected to Jesus—*on earth and in heaven*. St. Augustine and all the saints look down upon us and cheer us on; they know well the vices that beset us, and they also know the victory that awaits us if we persevere.

As with the example of St. Augustine, a saint is not one who never fell; a saint is one who got back up—again and again and again. This, too, can be our lot, if only we let the Lord completely into our lives, allowing him to be Lord of our entire minds and hearts.

Jesus as Our Model

The Christian life is a re-living of Christ's life—his life reproduced in us, as St. Paul states so vigorously: "It is no longer I who live, but Christ who lives in me" (Galatians 2:20). The mystery of Christianity comes down to the Holy Spirit reproducing Christ's life in us, as St. John Eudes captures here:

> We must continue to accomplish in ourselves the stages of Jesus' life and his mysteries and often to beg him to perfect and realize them in us and in his whole Church. ... For it is the plan of the Son of God to make us and the whole Church partake in his mysteries and to extend them to and continue them in us and in his whole Church. This is his plan for fulfilling his mysteries in us."[169]

Three time-tested practices for growing in conformity to Christ are *prayer, fasting,* and *almsgiving,* which we will explore in more detail in the following chapters.

We see these practices throughout the Old Testament, but our greatest model for these spiritual exercises is the Lord Jesus. He is the Father's champion—the ultimate spiritual athlete.

The Gospels show Jesus going out to pray (see Mark 1:35; Luke 5:16). Jesus himself fasted (see Matthew 4:2). And, as we will see, Jesus is the mercy expressed in almsgiving—the mercy of God poured out for us, both in his death and in the generous outpouring of his life before the Cross (see Luke 8:48; John 11:38–44).

Prayer, Fasting, and Almsgiving: Therapy and Training

We practice these exercises because we are Jesus' disciples. As the master did, the disciples do. But can we discern any deeper divine logic behind our Lord's clear exhortations about prayer, fasting, and almsgiving?

We have already seen that Divine Providence is the name we give to God's amazing way of leading all things to their ultimate perfection. It even has the power to take evil and use it despite itself to bring forth a greater good. The lingering wound from original sin—concupiscence—is one of our chief enemies, aided and abetted by the world and the devil. St. John describes concupiscence, the ongoing legacy of original sin, as manifesting itself in three forms:

> Do not love the world or the things in the world. If anyone loves the world, love for the Father is not in him. For all that is in the world, the *lust of the flesh* and the *lust of the eyes* and the *pride of life*, is not of the Father but is of the world.[170]
>
> —1 John 2:15–16; emphasis added

This triple form of concupiscence corresponds to the primordial temptation in the garden of Eden when Eve beheld the forbidden fruit: "So when the woman saw the tree was *good for food*, and that it was a *delight to the eyes*, and that the tree was to be desired *to make one wise*, she took of its fruit and ate" (Genesis 3:6; emphasis added).

John's "lust of the flesh" corresponds to the forbidden fruit as good "for food." This is a reference to our disordered carnal desires. The "lust of the eyes" matches the forbidden fruit as a "delight to the eyes." This refers to covetousness or greed.[171] Finally, the "pride of life" connects with the forbidden fruit as "desirable to make one wise." This expresses a desire for radical autonomy. This is the deadliest sin of all: a desire "to be like God, but without God." It is the capital sin of pride: the refusal to embrace one's status as a creature—the determination to usurp the place of the Creator.[172]

Here we see how the story of Adam and Eve is also every person's story.

The triple concupiscence described by St. John, corresponding to the very first temptation in Eden, refers to our disordered desires for *pleasure, possessions,* and *power.* They boil down to lust, greed, and pride.

Triple Concupiscence and Christ's Temptations in the Desert

The triple concupiscence described by St. John Eudes can be seen in Jesus' temptations in the desert (see Luke 4 and Matthew 4), where he relives both Israel's and humanity's stories, succeeding where each failed (see CCC 538). In Luke, the first temptation—to turn stones into bread—represents the *lust of the flesh.* The second temptation is to possess "all the kingdoms of the world," which expresses *greed.* And the third temptation is to test the Lord by throwing himself down and demonstrating his divine power, which is *pride.* As he overcomes the temptations, Jesus overcomes the triple concupiscence, undoing the sin of the garden by succeeding where primordial humanity failed. This victory in the desert anticipates Jesus' definitive victory over the Evil One on the Cross.

Here, we come to the underlying logic of *prayer, fasting,* and *almsgiving.* These three disciplines counter the triple concupiscence of our wounded nature: lust, greed, and pride.

- Prayer directly combats our inclination toward pride.
- Fasting directly combats the lust of the flesh.
- And almsgiving directly combats the "lust of the eyes" (greed).

The best way to overcome bad habits of vice is to practice the opposite virtues. We cannot simply "not do the bad"—we must practice the opposing good; we must replace the bad habit with a corresponding good habit. For this reason, God's prescription for overcoming lust, greed, and pride is to practice fasting, almsgiving, and prayer.

But here is where the mystery of Divine Providence manifests its amazing power and wisdom. Satan sought to infect humanity with his own pride. Tragically, Adam and Eve took the bait and were deeply wounded by sin, leaving us, their descendants, with the scar from the serpent's bite—this triple concupiscence. Prayer, fasting, and almsgiving are the spiritual therapy that the Divine Physician prescribes to help us regain our ability to walk with him. As we struggle against this resistance, our spiritual muscles grow stronger. We not only regain our ability to walk—striving against our adversaries, we exert ourselves against serious opponents and so gain strength and power that we never would have developed otherwise. God providentially uses our foes against themselves. The serpent's aim is to debilitate us; the Lord uses our struggles against the serpent to make us strong. Jesus Christ has conquered! He is not only our Redeemer but our physician and our trainer!

No Pain, No Gain

We do not really know what we are made of until we are *tested.* Every athlete knows that such testing often brings something out of us that we did not know we had—that is, it brings out a greatness that we would not have discovered otherwise. God "tests" us not so much to see if we will pass but to facilitate our transformation.

God wants us to become saints (see 1 Corinthians 1:2). More than just repenting of our sin, God wants to conquer the last vestiges of sin in us. He wants not only to forgive us but to heal and transform us.

Those things really worth having in life come at a price. Everywhere we turn, there are obstacles. If we surrender to these, we are overcome. If we push against them valiantly and unceasingly, persevering in prayer and other spiritual exercises, we will soon find ourselves developing the spiritual muscles called virtues. The Holy Spirit, our trainer in holiness, puts more weight on the bar only to make us stronger.

Hear, O Israel: The LORD our God is one LORD; and you shall love the LORD your God with all your heart, and with all your soul, and with all your might

— *Deuteronomy 6:4–5*

CHAPTER 14

Prayer, Liturgy, and Devotion

Most of us know that we need to pray more than we do. But just how literally are we supposed to take the command to pray *always*? (see 1 Thessalonians 5:17; Luke 18:1; Ephesians 6:18). For most of us, perpetual prayer is a long way off. How do we figure out the next best step in that direction? And if we do manage to carve out more time to spend with God, how should we fill that time?

Prayer and the Eucharist

First off, the Eucharist is the perfect prayer. For its power to be unlocked in our lives, however, it cannot be our only prayer. The soil must be tilled if the seed is to grow and bear fruit. First, we must pray before we attend Mass. In other words, we must come to Mass "pre-prayered." And then we must pray after Mass to give heartfelt thanks for the miracle that has occurred.

The Eucharistic liturgy is itself a school of prayer in which the Spirit and the Bride teach us to pray in our everyday lives. First, the Eucharist teaches us powerful principles about priorities and the structure of prayer. It all starts with *adoration and praise* (the *Gloria* we recite on most Sundays and feasts). It proceeds to *contrition*, an expression of sorrow for sin ("Lord, have mercy"). Then there is the very center of the Liturgy, which provides its name—the Eucharistic Prayer of *thanksgiving*. And toward the end of that prayer, there is *supplication* as the priest prays for the pope, the bishop, the deceased, and all who are present.[173]

There is a handy acronym to help us remember these different dimensions of prayer: *ACTS*, for adoration, contrition, thanksgiving, and supplication. Is it okay to ask for what we need? Of course. Jesus said, "Ask, and you will receive" (John 16:24). That is called *petition*, which is one aspect of supplication. Asking for what *others* may need is the other side of supplication, *intercession*.

But notice that asking God for things comes last in the list. Adoration, praise for who God is in himself, comes first. And thanksgiving for all that God has given is the central thing. Not to leave out contrition—we never have Mass without calling to mind our sins. But, in the Eucharist, we do not dwell on our sins very long. We say we are sorry, receive his pardon, and move on.[174] In Eucharistic worship, we look primarily to him, not to ourselves. Spending the lion's share of our prayer time focusing on who God is and the marvelous things he has done fills us with light and joy: "Look to him, and be radiant!" (Psalm 34:5). Conversely, dwelling on our sins, our needs, and the problems in the world that need fixing tends to make us miserable.

There is another key principle of prayer that the Liturgy teaches us. Prayer is conversation with God, and what God has to say is more important than anything we have to say. So, after some preliminary praise and contrition, we settle down and listen to God's Word. This is, in fact, the pattern for just about every liturgical celebration of the Catholic Church. Each one prominently features readings from Scripture.[175] God gave us two ears and one mouth for a reason: we are to listen twice as much as we speak.[176]

The Liturgical Year: The Sanctification of Time

The Church's liturgy, as we have seen, is not limited to the Eucharist and sacraments. The Word became flesh, which means God entered into time and sanctified it. The liturgical calendar is the Spirit working through the Church to make holy the natural cycle of the year.

The rhythm of the liturgical seasons provides a quiet yet colorful backdrop for our life of personal prayer. It is a ceaseless cycle of burrowing ever more deeply into the mystery of Christ. In Advent, we focus on hope; as Israel awaited the first coming of the messiah, so we await the second. In

Christmastide, we ponder the mystery of the Incarnation. In Lent, we go into the desert with Christ and accept the Church's forty-day fitness challenge—the spiritual version of spring training. In Holy Week, we mourn Christ's betrayal and suffering. From Easter through the Ascension, we rejoice in his resurrection. Between Ascension and Pentecost, we pray for a fresh outpouring of the Spirit—the promise of the Father. Each year, we go around again, but the cycle is more like a spiral than a circle. For each year, we penetrate more deeply into the mystery. Over time, for Christians who are truly seeking to live the liturgical year, it becomes the rhythm not only of their prayer but of their entire lives.

Punctuating the liturgical year like birthdays are the feast days of numerous saints. In fact, most feast days correspond to the day of a saint's death—that is, their birth into eternal life. We celebrate their witness as that of older brothers and sisters in the Faith who have run the race and now cheer us on.

The Hours and Praying Always

The cycle of each day is also sanctified by the Church's Liturgy of the Hours.

In the days of ancient Israel, Jews recited the ancient *Shema* twice daily: "Hear [*Shema*], O Israel: the LORD our God is one LORD, and you shall love the LORD your God with all your heart, and with all your soul, and with all your might" (Deuteronomy 6:4–5). Set times of prayer also correlated with the times of the Temple sacrifices (see Daniel 6:10). These ancient Jewish practices are the origin of what became the Liturgy of the Hours, the Church's prayer throughout set hours of the day.[177]

The psalms—"the masterwork of prayer of the Old Testament" (CCC 2585)—became the backbone of the Hours, along with the great New Testament Canticles of Zechariah (see Luke 1:68–79), Mary (see Luke 1:46–55), and Simeon (see Luke 2:25–32) and the greatest canticles of the Old Testament, such as that of the three young men in the fiery furnace (see Daniel 3:29–68).[178]

This continuous sanctification of day and night is the Church's official work of fulfilling the command to pray always. The Liturgy of the Hours was originally the prayer not of the clergy but of the whole Church. It was done first in homes, but, as soon as Christianity became legal, the liturgy was done publicly in churches with large daily attendance for Lauds (Morning Prayer) before work and Vespers (Evening Prayer) after work. In fact, many of the greatest homilies of the Fathers of the Church were preached not at Mass but at Lauds or Vespers. When literacy was lost in the "dark ages," the hours became associated with monastic and clerical life because few laity could read or understand the Latin of the liturgy.

But the Second Vatican Council recognized that this treasure needed to be restored and become once again the common patrimony of the entire Church. Accordingly, the Divine Office, as it is also called, was reformed in the Roman rite to be more concise and was made available in the vernacular, the common language of the people.

When my (Marcellino's) conversion began at age sixteen, my spiritual director insisted that I begin to pray the Liturgy of the Hours. I was intimidated, to say the least. But, trusting his judgment, I dived in. I started slowly. Morning Prayer, which focuses on praise and thanks, took ten to fifteen minutes to pray. *That's doable*, I thought. Once I had that under my belt, I added the Office of Readings, which contains not only a page from Scripture but one from a saint or Father of the Church. All the readings are coordinated with the seasons and the saints' days. Thus, the Office of Readings became my crash course in the Catholic Tradition.

I then added Vespers in the evening. This prayer features psalms that express trust in God and culminates in praying the Magnificat with Mary and the entire Church in heaven and on earth. Finally, I tried Compline (Night Prayer), the seven-minute prayer that completes the day—its very last prayer being the Hail, Holy Queen. It is like being tucked into bed by our Blessed Mother, Mary. By this time, I realized that the Liturgy of the Hours is one of the Church's greatest gifts to her children.

When my wife and I were blessed with twins, our times of quiet, focused prayer mostly disappeared. We struggled to hang onto Morning Prayer, with one parent covering while the other prayed. We had learned a sung Compline at a monastic retreat one time and decided to sing this to our kids as a lullaby. The children were so comforted by the chant and Our

Lady's night-time embrace that they have all decided, now that they are parents, to sing the same Compline to their children each night.

The Liturgy of the Hours is truly liturgy—a priestly act of Christ our head and his entire body in heaven and on earth. By praying it together in our home, even at the bedside of our children, we are immersing ourselves in the cosmic reality of the heavenly liturgy. We are fulfilling our call to be the domestic church, consecrating our home as a place of liturgical worship. This liturgical prayer, together with the sacraments, is the chief conduit of the Catholic Tradition that comes down to us from the apostles. While the time will eventually come for older children and adults to study the truth in a formal fashion, in the liturgy we are formed and fed by the truth. We absorb it as if by osmosis.

When the COVID pandemic prevented my (Andrew's) family from attending Mass for a while, we prayed the hours together—Morning, Evening, and Night prayer. While we longed to get back to Mass, this was a powerful time of prayer for our family as we experienced the Church's liturgy forming our minds and hearts in a new way. While we were not able to keep all of this up permanently when regular schedules resumed, we have kept up the practice of praying Night Prayer as a family. It is amazing how even the younger children respond when time is set aside for the Lord. (As any parent knows, their spiritual questions can sometimes be astounding!)

If you have never explored the Liturgy of the Hours, the important thing— as with anything in the life of prayer—is just to get started. You do not need to buy a book or take a class to do it. If you have a computer or smartphone, you can use an app that will display the prayers of the day on your screen. Want to pray Morning Prayer? Just select it and pray. Compline? Do the same.[179] Just start with one of the hours, either Morning Prayer, Evening Prayer, the Office of Readings, Midday Prayer, or Night Prayer. When you can do more, add another.

The feast days through the year and the Hours through the day provide a stability to my life that I just could not live without. Over the years, they have proved to be, for me and my family, one of the Church's greatest gifts.

Lectio Divina

Have you ever gone to Mass and found that one particular Scripture just stands out and grabs you? That is most likely the Holy Spirit drawing you to come back to that reading after Mass and dig deeper. The same thing happens when you pray the Liturgy of the Hours. A certain line of a psalm just lights up. So, after Mass or Vespers in the earliest days of the Church, a monk would pick up the sacred page and look for that text that stood out during the liturgy. He would then chew on it, "ruminating," trying to extract every bit of nourishment that he could from it. He would read and re-read it, sometimes memorize it, meditate on it, and use it as a springboard to more contemplative prayer.[180] St. Benedict called this process of assimilating the Word of God "divine reading" or, in Latin, *lectio divina*.

Scripture has a quasi-sacramental structure. It is a sacred place where we meet the Lord who wishes to speak to us personally. The Scriptures are the living Word of God. They are *in-breathed* by the Holy Spirit and so become a temple of that Spirit who wants to communicate his transforming power to those who come to meet him in the sacred page. *Lectio divina* reminds us that we come to Scripture not so much for *in*-formation as for *formation* or, indeed, *trans*-formation.

If you do not already have a prayer journal, try starting one. When you are able to make time for *lectio divina*, whether daily or periodically, write down the Scripture you are drawn to ponder and the insights that come as you pray and meditate on it. Periodically, review your journal, highlighter in hand. Over time, you will see patterns emerge that will indicate what God is saying to you. It is amazing what we forget over time when we do not write things down—how we felt, what we were thinking; if we take the time to journal, we often gain powerful perspective when we go back to old entries and can grasp larger movements of God's work in our lives.

The Rosary

The sacraments, the liturgical year, and the Liturgy of the Hours are liturgical prayer—the public, official prayer of Christ our head and his entire body.

Lectio divina is what is called popular or devotional prayer. It is a personal act of "owning" and internalizing what is received in the liturgy.

Another great devotional prayer that does the same is the Rosary. This prayer actually arose as a way for those who could not read and, therefore, could not profitably participate in the Liturgy of the Hours. The original 150 Hail Marys of the fifteen-decade Rosary stood in for the 150 psalms.

But the Rosary is more than a vocal recitation of memorized prayers. It is primarily a prayer of meditation, like *lectio divina*. Like the liturgical year, it meditates on the entire mystery of Christ—his incarnation, public ministry, suffering, and resurrection into glory—together with Mary, the first Christian contemplative. Luke emphasizes twice in the same chapter that Mary pondered all these things in her heart (see Luke 2:19, 51). Mary's focus was not on herself but on her Son. As Pope St. John Paul II put it, "To recite the Rosary is nothing other than to *contemplate with Mary the face of Christ*" (*Rosarium Virginis Mariae*, 3), since Mary always points to her Son and continues to tell us to "do whatever he tells you" (John 2:5).

Each decade begins with the Lord's Prayer, the prayer he taught us, and his name is the "center of gravity" of each Hail Mary that follows it (*Rosarium Virginis Mariae*, 33).

The key to getting the most out of the Rosary is to make it truly meditative. Many have found it helpful to read a brief Scripture passage before each mystery, making it a "Scriptural Rosary."[181] This helps us channel our focus and enter more fully into the mystery. It also helps us to imagine the setting—the people present, the sounds and smells—as if we were watching the events unfold before our eyes.

The Jesus Prayer

The Rosary is the greatest devotional prayer of the Western Church. Though not part of the liturgy, it draws its inspiration from it and leads back to it. The same can be said for the greatest devotional prayer of the East, the Jesus prayer. It consists simply of repeating the name of Jesus; as the *Catechism* says, "The invocation of the holy name of Jesus is the simplest way of praying always" (CCC 2668).

This prayer has various wordings, the simplest of which is simply the name of Jesus. But, usually, the prayer includes a confession of faith and a supplication such as "Lord Jesus Christ, son of the living God, have mercy on me, a sinner." This confession of Jesus Christ as Lord (see Philippians 2:11) is the central act of Christian faith; the plea for mercy, which resounds in the liturgies of both East and West, is an act of humility and an invitation for the Lord to heal and transform us. It echoes the prayer of the tax collector in Luke 18:13 as well as the pleas of many who were healed by Jesus: the two blind men of Jericho—"Have mercy on us, Son of David" (Matthew 20:30); the blind Bartimaeus (see Mark 10:48); the ten lepers (see Luke 17:13); and the mother whose daughter was possessed by an evil spirit (see Matthew 15:22).

In the East, a beautiful discipline developed of reciting this to the rhythm of one's heartbeat and breathing. Inhaling while saying, "Lord Jesus Christ, Son of the Living God," allows the Son to breathe life into us; exhaling while saying, "Have mercy on me, a sinner," is giving him our sin and brokenness. Many in the course of Christian history have endeavored to repeat this prayer so often that it becomes a constant rhythm in the background throughout their waking hours. The goal is to thus make it "the prayer of the heart."[182]

The Jesus prayer is also seen as a gateway to contemplative prayer, to resting in inner quiet in the presence of the Lord. To whatever degree you can incorporate it into your life, it can become a way to refresh your connection to the Lord throughout the day, wherever you are and whatever you may be doing.

The Jesus prayer can also be a powerful antidote when we are faced with temptation—after all, there is power in the very name of Jesus (see Philippians 2:9–11).

We Dare to Call Him Father

As sons and daughters in Christ, we now pray with a "filial boldness."[183] The letter to the Hebrews uses the Greek word *parrhesia* to describe this newfound intimacy and bold confidence we have with the Father through Jesus: "Let us then with confidence [*parrhesia*] draw near to the throne of grace" (Hebrews 4:16). In other words, we do not pray as slaves or even employees. God invites us to approach him in a manner that transcends the prerogative of any creature—as beloved sons and daughters.

When we pray in Jesus' name, we enter the Father's eternal embrace of his divine Son. The Father loves us in the Son—that is, he loves us *as he loves his only begotten Son.*[184] This may sound too good to be true, but it is the supernatural mystery of faith—the Good News of the Gospel. The deepest desire of our hearts is to be accepted, cherished, and perfectly loved by someone. How extraordinary that this love comes to us from the Creator of the Universe himself, who has made us his sons and daughters!

The *Catechism*, following Hebrews, describes profoundly this filial boldness: "*Parrhesia* [is] straightforward simplicity, filial trust, joyous assurance, humble boldness, *the certainty of being loved*" (CCC 2778; emphasis added). This is the newness wrought in Christ Jesus, which is ours to experience through a life of regular prayer.

Eucharistic Adoration

Lectio divina enables us to take the bread of the Word, received in the liturgy, and hold that Word in an extended moment of contemplation. Eucharistic Adoration does the same thing but with the Bread of Life, which is the Blessed Sacrament. Adoration before the Eucharistic Host prepares our spiritual appetite for the feast of faith. After the Eucharist, it serves as an opportunity to digest and assimilate the Bread of Life. As many have found, just as basking in the sun makes us tan, so, too, our presence before the gaze of the eternal Son in Adoration helps us to take on his complexion—his very mind and heart.

When it comes to Adoration, there are two extremes to avoid. Some people fill Adoration with so many devotions and prayers that there is no opportunity to rest silently in Jesus' presence. Others go to the opposite extreme, thinking that quiet gazing upon him in the sanctuary should be the only activity. Most of us are ill-equipped to have nothing but the tabernacle or the monstrance as our prayer focus. We need a Scripture passage or a prayer to distract us from our distractions and bring our attention back to prayer. It is helpful to have your Bible or some spiritual reading on hand as a springboard for prayer or a home base to which you can return when your mind has been wandering. Two of my favorites are Psalm 63 ("My soul thirsts for you") and Psalm 84 ("How lovely is your dwelling place, O LORD of hosts!").

Pilgrimage and Retreats

Prayer is like breathing. You need to do it all the time. But, sometimes, you need to sit back and take a really deep breath.

Special time with more extensive focus on prayer, commonly called a retreat, has always proved to be an important part of the spiritual life. Sometimes, you may have the opportunity to do a weekend or a single overnight retreat. Seize the opportunity if you can. This has been a regular feature of my own life for decades. But, when I am not able to do this, I take a day or a morning, pack up my Bible and my journal, and just spend extended time in a monastery chapel that is just far enough away from home to help me leave my work and cares behind. My phone is turned off, and I am at the Lord's disposal. I always emerge from such times with him reenergized and with a new sense of direction and purpose.

A special form of retreat is a pilgrimage—a regular and required part of life for Jesus as a Jewish man. He, together with his family first, and then later his disciples, walked almost 150 miles round trip to Jerusalem at least three times a year to take part in week-long festivals there. We are a pilgrim people called to pursue God, not just believe in him. So getting up and going to a special place, hallowed by his presence, is a special act of renewal and dedication that can be a game-changer, a true mountain-top experience. The destination could be Rome, Jerusalem, Krakow, or

Lourdes. Or it could be a nearby monastery or your diocesan cathedral. The important thing is that you are pursuing him and honoring him in a place consecrated to him.

Other Devotions and Sacramentals

There are many other kinds of popular prayer and devotions: chaplets, like that of the Divine Mercy; novenas, which recall the nine days of the apostles' vigil for the coming of the Spirit at Pentecost; the stations of the Cross; or meetings for informal song and prayer. And, in all these popular devotions, many images and objects, blessed by a priest or deacon, serve as visible, tangible aids to prayer. These objects include holy water, rosaries, chaplets, scapulars and medals, icons, and statues. Setting up a prayer corner in your home with such blessed objects can be a great help to personal and family prayer.

In popular Catholic speech, such blessed objects are often called sacramentals. In fact, though, sacramentals are the liturgical prayers of blessing, not the things so blessed. The items are simply devotional objects. After their dedication to divine use, blessed items should be used reverently and treated with respect. They are a sign that the Word indeed became flesh and forever makes use of the tangible, visible things of creation to help us grow in holiness.

Some sacramentals are for the dedication of churches, and some occur when a religious makes solemn vows. Funerals and graveside services are also special blessings. Bishops, priests, or deacons preside at such blessings (see CCC 1669).

Since all Christians are called to consecrate the world to God,[185] the Second Vatican Council mandated a revision of the sacramentals of the Roman rite so that there are numerous blessings over which lay people may preside. As lay people, we do not impart blessings in the name of the Church as clergy do. But we are authorized to call down God's blessing, directing the intercession of the entire Church in a special moment of spiritual intensity. There are blessings of the sick, blessings on birthdays, blessings for a newly engaged couple, blessings for a manger, an Advent wreath, and a Christmas tree, and special table blessings for feasts. The blessings help us make our homes true domestic churches and extend the reach of the sacred liturgy into every dimension of human life. The blessing services are short and include appropriate readings from Scripture and beautiful prayers from the heart of the Church.[186]

The Next Best Step

People who are determined to exercise may have one of several reactions when they first walk into a fitness club filled with all sorts of exercise equipment. They may be overwhelmed by all the possibilities and, indecisive about which machines to use, freeze and do nothing. Or they may attack several different machines in their first fitness session, wake up extremely sore the next day, and never go back to the gym. Or they might come up with a plan to start somewhere, modestly, with just a few repetitions of one or two exercises at low intensity. These people come back, expand their program, and, if they persevere, reach their fitness goals.

As Catholics, we have many ways of prayer to choose from. Ask the Holy Spirit which one is the next best step for you right now to grow as a woman or man of prayer. Trust that the Spirit is attracting you to the way of prayer that is good for you now. And then get started and do your best to be *consistent*.

As with exercise, so, too, with prayer: Be zealous but also be *patient* with yourself. Slow and steady wins the race!

CHAPTER 15

Fasting: Making Room for God

Reaching out to the Lord in prayer requires effort and energy. It certainly qualifies as a form of spiritual exercise. As we have seen, it is indeed the most important one of all. But no fitness regimen can bypass the issue of diet. You can exercise a great deal, but if you do not control what you put in your mouth, you will never get control of your weight or your health.

The same is true in the spiritual realm. "Walking in faith" is not a casual stroll after a big dinner. The same apostle who refers to "walking by faith" urges us to break into a trot and, ultimately, a sprint:

> Do you not know that in a race all the runners compete, but only one receives the prize? So run that you may obtain it. Every athlete exercises self-control in all things. They do it to receive a perishable wreath, but we an imperishable. Well, I do not run aimlessly, I do not box as one beating the air; but I pommel my body and subdue it, lest after preaching to others I myself should be disqualified.

> —1 Corinthians 9:24–27

St. Paul wanted to know Christ and the power flowing from his resurrection. But he also wanted to know how to share in Christ's suffering, being formed into the pattern of his death (see Philippians 3:10). Prayer connects us to the risen Christ, our life. Fasting is a sharing in his death. It is the mortification, or crucifying, of our desire for bodily pleasure that we might run the race to win.

In this chapter, we will discuss the role of fasting in Catholic life, beginning with abstaining from food and drink. But we will not stop there. Applying the discipline of fasting to our desires for pleasures beyond food may be even more important to our spiritual health.

We cannot be filled with the fullness of Christ unless we first empty ourselves. "Blessed are those who hunger and thirst for righteousness, for they shall be satisfied" (Matthew 5:6). Fasting, in essence, is making room for God.

Fasting in Scripture

In the Old Testament, fasting is sometimes a way of mourning a death.[187] It can signify repentance as a way for the people to humble themselves before God, acknowledging total dependence on him. This is the meaning of the Ash Wednesday custom of receiving ashes on the head (or forehead) while fasting as we hear the lines from Genesis, "Remember man that you are dust and unto dust you shall return" or "Repent, and believe in the Gospel" (*Roman Missal*; see Genesis 3:19; Mark 1:5).

Times of national crisis were also times of fasting.[188] And, on the Day of Atonement, fasting was mandatory (see Leviticus 23:27).

In the New Testament, Jesus is very clear about fasting, giving direction not *if* we fast but *when* we do so (see Matthew 6:18). He also speaks of a future time when his disciples will fast (see Matthew 9:15).

While Jesus certainly teaches us to fast, he also warns us against turning it into an act of pride and using it to draw attention to ourselves (see Matthew 6:16–18). We can also distort it by treating it as a form of *dieting*. If losing weight and becoming more fit better serves the kingdom, then great. But when our dieting and training are carried out simply to impress others, they become acts of pride and vanity. Self-denial has spiritual value only when it is carried out for the glory of God.

While fasting can be a sign of repentance, it can also be part of preparation and consecration for an important mission as it was for Esther (see Esther 4:16) and Judith (see Judith 4:9).[189] This is why Jesus, though sinless, fasted in the wilderness, preparing for his public ministry and offering his forty-day sacrifice in homage to his Father and in intercession for us. In his deflection of Satan's temptations, Jesus makes clear that fasting is an act of worship because it is a proclamation that we need God more than food: Man does not live by bread alone but by every word that comes from the mouth of God (see Matthew 4:4; Luke 4:4).[190] Jesus also makes clear that fasting is a way to intensify our prayers of supplication, whether they be petitions for ourselves or intercession for others. Notice how he responds when the disciples fail to deliver a boy with a demon: "This kind cannot be driven out by anything but prayer and fasting" (Mark 9:29).

Fasting in the Church's History and Liturgy

Since Baptism is entry into the death and resurrection of Christ, it became customary in the early Church for most Baptisms to take place at the Easter Vigil. The baptismal fast went from three to forty days in honor of Christ's fast in the wilderness. And the entire Church fasted with those awaiting Baptism, both as a renewal of their own baptismal commitment and as intercession for those trying to wrestle free from Satan's dominion. Thus, the season of Lent was born.

By the fourth century, a period of fasting prior to the Sunday Eucharist had become widespread. The obligatory pre-Communion fast in the Roman rite today is minimal, but it still serves to remind us that we need to empty ourselves to make room for the Bread of Heaven.

Fasting was also a regular weekly discipline in the early Church. The *Didache* shows that, just as Christians continued the Jewish practice of prayer several times a day, they also continued fasting twice a week. But Christians were encouraged to fast on different days than the Jews. Instead of Tuesdays and Thursdays, Christians were to fast on Wednesdays and Fridays (see *Didache*, 8). Fridays became a weekly memorial of the Lord's death, while Sunday, the supreme Eucharistic day, was the commemoration of his resurrection. Even now, the Eastern churches keep Wednesday and Friday as penitential days. In the Roman rite, Friday is traditionally a day to abstain from meat, although Catholics in the United States are free to substitute some other form of penance on Fridays outside of Lent.

So fasting as a penitential practice follows the same rule as prayer: it flows from the liturgy and back to it. Like the liturgical year, there is both a weekly and yearly cycle of fasting that we do together as a family in sync with the liturgy. But then we are called to interiorize and personalize fasting, as we do prayer, under the guidance of the Holy Spirit.

Mourning over Sin

Jesus says, "Blessed are those who mourn, for they shall be comforted" (Matthew 5:4). Traditionally, "mourning" here has been understood in relation to our sin.[191] Pope Benedict XVI distinguished between the *mourning of Peter* after he denied Jesus and the *mourning of Judas* after his betrayal of the Lord. Peter's mourning brought about the conversion of a saint, whereas Judas's ended in tragic despair:

> There are two kinds of mourning. The first is the kind that has lost hope, that has become mistrustful of love and of truth, and that therefore eats away and destroys man from within. *But there is also the mourning occasioned by the shattering encounter with truth*, which leads man to undergo conversion and to resist evil. This mourning heals, because it teaches man to hope and to love again. Judas is an example of the first kind of mourning: Struck with horror at his own fall, he no longer dares to hope and hangs himself in despair. Peter is an example of the second kind: *Struck by the Lord's gaze, he bursts into healing tears that plow up the soil of his soul.* He begins anew and is himself renewed.[192]

Coming to grips with our own brokenness, we enter the poverty of spirit—that is, the humility—necessary for life in the kingdom of God (see Matthew 5:3). In other words, in mourning our brokenness, we recognize our need for God and his grace. This humility opens us up to God's transforming power.

Becoming Perfect in Christ

Jesus calls us to be "perfect" as his heavenly father is perfect (see Matthew 5:48). The Greek word for "perfect" here is *teleios*. The Hebrew roots of Jesus' words connote "wholeness" or "completion." Sin has wounded us, and we need not just forgiveness but *healing* and *transformation* as well. Jesus here calls us to become *whole* and *complete* by being transformed by the power of the Holy Spirit.[193]

The language of being "perfect" shows up again in the story of the rich young man (Matthew 19:16–22). In this encounter, Jesus clearly connects salvation to the keeping of the commandments. When the young man asks "Teacher, what good deed must I do, to have eternal life?" (v. 16). Jesus replies, "If you would enter life, *keep the commandments*" (v. 17; emphasis added). Jesus runs through a summary of the Ten Commandments, and the young man says, "All these I have observed; what do I still lack?" (v. 20). So Jesus responds, "If you would be perfect [*teleios*], go, sell what you possess and give to the poor, and you will have treasure in heaven; and come, follow me" (v. 21). Famously, the young man goes away sad, "for he had great possessions" (v. 22).

Pope St. John Paul II saw in this young man the story of every person.[194] The young man seems to be like a lot of us—basically a "good guy" but afraid to go "all-in" with Jesus, afraid to let Jesus take the reins of his life. He is too attached to the comforts and familiarity of his life and is, therefore, afraid to let go.

What attachments are holding us back from greater intimacy with Jesus? Where are we afraid to let him in? What areas of my life am I afraid to hand over to him and place fully under his lordship?

Interestingly, the next chapter in Matthew (chapter 20) gives us the parable of the laborers in the vineyard, some of whom arrive late, at the eleventh hour. It suggests that hope remains for the rich young man—and for us. It is never too late to give our lives completely to Jesus.

Training in Temperance?

In itself, pleasure is good and is part of God's created order. Rightly ordered, it encourages behavior that leads to life and health (e.g., eating, procreation, etc.). It is intended as a means to an end. But we have a natural tendency to become attached to it and, given our inheritance of sin, it easily dominates our lives. Satan cannot create an ounce of pleasure, but he is adept at using it as bait, tempting us to indulge in it either excessively or outside of its proper context. In these ways, pleasure enslaves.

We all know how easily we can become attached, even addicted, to just about any pleasure. Fasting is a way to "cut the cord," to break our attachments to pleasure so that Satan cannot use them to entrap us and lead us to sin: "Truly, truly, I say to you, every one who commits sin is a slave to sin" (John 8:34).

In other words, to retrain ourselves and reclaim our free and balanced enjoyment of the good things God gives us, we go without some legitimate pleasures on occasion. By practicing self-denial, we grow in self-mastery and freedom.

As a former college athlete (Andrew), I found these ideas instrumental in my conversion. I knew that I would look down on a fellow teammate who could not finish a given workout. But what about someone who did not have the self-discipline to say no to an illicit pleasure? All of a sudden, I was able to connect the dots: *The person overcome by passion and unable to control himself is no different than my hypothetical teammate who couldn't finish his sprints*; both lacked the discipline required for self-mastery. As my conversion came to a head, I knew that if I could not deny myself—if I could not attain self-mastery—then what could my yes to anyone or anything ever really mean? As I came to see, self-mastery is the prerequisite of self-gift; self-mastery makes true love possible. Without self-mastery, our efforts to "love" become forms of self-love in disguise.

In this sense, fasting is not an end in itself; its value is that it helps us make room for God. By mastering our thirst for comfort, we learn to "hunger and thirst for righteousness" (Matthew 5:6). Fasting strengthens us so that we do not become the hypothetical undisciplined teammate mentioned above, unwilling to be steadfast and firm in pursuit of the good, especially when things get hard.

Tempered glass, which is heat-treated, is four to five times stronger than normal glass and much less likely to break under the force of a blow. Similarly, the temperate person accepts periods of discomfort to become stronger, more balanced, and more resilient.

The virtue of temperance is a little like chips and salsa, the first thing usually brought out when you eat in a Mexican restaurant. If you are hungry, you might ask for an additional bowl of chips, and then another—and maybe another after that. If you continue like this, what happens when the meal comes out? You are already full!

The same is true in life: if we fill up on the chips and salsa, we miss out on the main course. Temperance is the virtue that helps us (metaphorically and really) not fill up on chips and salsa. It is not about suppressing desire but moderating it. By preserving right order and balance, temperance helps us live more fully; it helps us get the most out of life. In C.S. Lewis's words, temperance is about the ability to go "the right length and no further."[195]

Temperance requires a certain *firmness*, a strength of character that the hypothetical teammate lacked. Without this firmness, every virtue eventually falters at its testing point. As Lewis observed, even "Pilate was merciful till it became risky."[196]

When tested, will our character seek the good—even when it gets uncomfortable? As disciples, do we have the firmness needed to live a life of integrity all the way through to the end? Are we willing and able to do so *when no one is watching?*

Fasting is a powerful way to prepare for these moments before they arise.

Joyful Fasting

To be spiritually fruitful, fasting must be done with "cheerfulness of heart,"[197] not in a dramatic and gloomy fashion like the hypocrites Jesus condemns (see Matthew 6:16). For this reason, fasting is often best done in moderation—and without complaining.

In other words, our fasting should not make the people around us miserable; our fasting should not become *their* mortification! This is where humility comes in: we should not take on more than we can handle *joyfully*. A moderate fast in which we maintain our cheerful availability to those around us is better than a "heroic" fast that makes us insufferable. If the discomfort of our fast becomes the overwhelming focus of our conversation and thought, something is probably off.

Fasting from Media

Virtue (and fasting in particular) is about restoring the center of gravity in our lives. It is not just about our actions but very much about our hearts and all that clamors for our allegiance.

When Jesus says, "Blessed are the *pure* in heart" (Matthew 5:8; emphasis added), he calls us to an *undivided* heart. We all worship something; we all have a matter of ultimate concern. To see what it is, all we have to do is look at our planners and notice how we spend our *time* and *money* as well as our emotional and psychological energy.

When it comes to food, the impact of vice is more varied than we realize. Take gluttony, for instance: This vice concerns not just quantity but also the temptation to be overly picky—or the need to have just the right foods prepared in an overly precise way.[198] In this way, even a person who does not eat a lot of food can become a slave to their appetites.

In a similar way, excessive use of social media or devotion to a hobby may become the "center" of our lives in an imbalanced way. Occasional fasting from such activities can help us refocus and re-center our lives in God. C.S. Lewis captures the need for a broader view of temperance that extends beyond physical desires:

> One great piece of mischief has been done by the modern restriction of the word Temperance to the question of drink. It helps people to forget that you can be just as intemperate about lots of other things. A man

who makes his golf or his motor-bicycle the center of his life, or a woman who devotes all her thoughts to clothes or bridge or her dog is being just as "intemperate" as someone who gets drunk every evening. Of course, it does not show on the outside so easily: bridge-mania or golf-mania do not make you fall down in the middle of the road. But God is not deceived by externals.[199]

The key is this: When we put God first—not just in word, but in action and thought—then secondary things fall into their proper places. But when secondary things become the center of our lives, our ability to love wanes, we become centered on self, and our lives often implode.

In my Christian Moral Life course at Benedictine College, I (Andrew) typically assign students a forty-eight-hour fast from social media and phones (except for making and receiving phone calls). Not unexpectedly, students complain about the assignment at first. In their reflections afterward, however, they are often surprised by how difficult—and how *liberating*—the exercise became by day two. On a fairly consistent basis, they report better sleep, reduced anxiety, better conversations, and increased productivity. They also report being surprised at how often other people were on their phones. Apparently, only when they stepped away from their phones did they notice how pervasive phone addiction is in the lives of others! It is surprising just how many students express thanks for the assignment and want to do a similar fast again in the future.

We often need to step away from something before we see how much control it really has over us. This is where occasional fasting can be pivotal, not only from food but from anything that tends to dominate our minds and hearts.

Fasting from News

One perennial modern challenge is the desire to "stay informed" about the pressing issues of the day and yet retain interior peace and focus on the Lord. Many people have noticed that American news sources tend to induce a sense of anger, panic, and even despair. This may be because the angrier and more afraid we become, the more we tune in to them. This may or may not be intentional on the part of news stations. But the real question is what is it doing to our spiritual lives, and who is forming our minds and hearts?

We want to have fully Catholic lenses with which to see the world. At a basic level, this means that election cycles and economic patterns are not the *most* important things—yet they are what get the lion's share of coverage. They are important, of course, but we should ask ourselves what we are so afraid of missing out on that we feel compelled to tune in every day (or even multiple times a day).

Is it possible that this stems in part from *vanity* (we do not want to be out of the loop in conversations at work)? Or could it be about *power* (we want to dominate a co-worker or family member who holds a different view)? Or do we have a restless and unhealthy addiction to anything "new," like the latest gossip? If anything is really that significant, do we really think we would not find out about it within a few days?

Lastly, what is the opportunity cost in terms of our time and emotional energy? Could we have used the time we spend watching and reacting to the news in other ways? For example, are we reading God's Word with as much focus and zeal as we are paying attention to other things? Do we want our coworkers and family members to know *Jesus* as much as we want them to see things our way politically?

Fasting from Our Own Will

One of our strongest appetites is for getting our own way. God created us free, which is certainly a great gift and responsibility. Yet, often in life, duty or charity dictate that we yield to the preferences of another person (e.g., a spouse, family member, army officer, or boss). Religious (e.g., nuns, monks, friars, and priests) often remark that *obedience* is the hardest of their vows—far more so than chastity or poverty. Dying to our own *will* is often more challenging than dying to our immediate desire for physical comfort and pleasure.

Sometimes, the challenge is to accept unexpected circumstances, as when a change in the weather or car trouble gets in the way of our plans. This brings to mind Jesus' invitation to us to pick up our cross daily (see Luke

9:23). The cross is where our will and God's will intersect. The Council of Trent says that this is the supreme test of our hearts, calling our patient acceptance of trials we do not choose "the most forceful proof of love."[200]

Light from the Gulag

In the darkening decade of the 1930s, Pope Pius XI appealed to seminarians to volunteer for missionary work in communist Russia. A Polish-American Jesuit studying for the priesthood, Walter Ciszek, responded to the call.[201] After training in Rome for this mission, Fr. Ciszek was sent to serve in eastern Poland because it was deemed too dangerous to go into the Soviet Union at the time.[202] Ciszek arrived in 1938. With war on the horizon, many of his Polish parishioners left for Russia, finding work in the Ural mountains.[203] Ciszek went with them, thinking that this was his chance to finally be a missionary to Russia. He was quickly arrested as a spy, however, and subjected to fifteen years of grueling labor, little food, and frequent torture in Soviet prison camps.

Instead of falling into bitter resentment and despair, Fr. Ciszek became increasingly convinced that, despite appearances to the contrary, God was at work: "I grew firmer in my conviction that *whatever* happened in my life was nothing else than a reflection of God's will for me. And He would protect me."[204] He observed, "What was there to fear so long as I did his will? Not death. Not failure, except the failure to do his will. ... [This] was my greatest joy and the source of tremendous interior strength."[205]

Fr. Ciszek was able to accept everything—the good, the bad, the ugly, and the disappointing—as a mysterious "gift" from the Lord, perceiving in each gift (however bleak it might look to human eyes) a call to offer it back to the Father as a holy sacrifice.

To do this with peace and joy—instead of resentment and bitterness—is truly heroic.

We might not be enslaved in a communist gulag, but we can imitate Fr. Ciszek's example by embracing the trials of a given day and offering them back to the Lord as a pleasing sacrifice. Like Fr. Ciszek, we can see all things, especially those we would never have chosen for ourselves, as mysterious gifts from the Father. In this way, we will retain our sense of joy and gratitude—and we will dramatically increase our ability to love those around us because we will have avoided the trap of self-absorption and excessive self-pity.

As we will see in the next chapter, fasting and giving alms are closely connected. In both practices, we realign our hearts to God and so become more sensitive to the needs of those around us. And the resources we free up as we fast—our time and money in particular—become available to them in the alms we give and the mercy we share.

In closing, here are some practical "tips" for making fasting a regular part of our lives and, thereby, strengthening our ability to love, even when it hurts:

- Occasional, moderate fasting from something that is relatively small but which we enjoy a great deal (e.g., ketchup, salt, soda, cream or sugar in coffee, etc.);

- Fasting from looking at our phones during meals with others;

- Fasting from needing to have the last word (perhaps especially on social media);

- Fasting from our favorite TV or news show;

- Fasting from the radio in the car (or perhaps one way of our commute to work);

- Perhaps designating a certain time slot to check social media, and fasting from it at all other hours of the day;

- Having the humility to get all the sleep one needs in order to live well and with charity (thus fasting from extra "productivity" and ambition);

- On Friday, the memorial of the Lord's passion, replacing lunch with either some extra prayer time or a noon Mass, or, alternately, fasting until noon, or until 3 pm, the hour that our Lord expired on the cross, or until dinner.

CHAPTER 16

Almsgiving: A Lifestyle of Mercy

The entire story of the Bible is about giving. Creation is itself a pure gift from God—a testimony to divine generosity. And, then, when humanity thumbed its nose at him, he gave them the even greater gift of salvation through his only begotten Son. That Son, giving the last drop of his blood, gave also to his disciples his body and his Spirit. Finally, the Holy Spirit, the Lord and Giver of life, proceeded to give us life plus every good gift to sustain that life.

The Eucharist is the greatest gift of them all: the source and summit of the Christian experience in this world. But it does not exhaust Christian life and experience. It must bear fruit. The ultimate goal of the gift is to make those who receive it givers. If God is love, which translates into pure generosity, then we who are divinized by the Spirit are being transformed into those who love and who give. Christ working through us means Christ giving through us. As Jesus said, "Without cost you have received; without cost you are to give" (Matthew 10:8; NABRE).

The term *charity* in common parlance refers to a material gift to those in need. But charity means more than giving dollars. It means giving of one*self*. Charity (*agape*) is the love among the three Persons of the Trinity, who give themselves to one another eternally. This love led the Father to give the world his Son. This is the love of Christ who on the Cross gives himself completely. This is the gift of the Spirit who, in giving us himself, gives us the power to love as God loves. Clearly, to be sons and daughters of the Father—to be Christians—means to learn to give ourselves away in very real and practical ways.

Giving in the Old Testament

From the beginning, God was training his people to be givers. The biblical tradition of the tithe is founded on the generosity of God: The land is a gift for the people of God, redeemed out of slavery in Egypt. The people of God are to imitate this generosity of God (see Leviticus 19:2, 9). The tithe supported the Levites, who had no land inheritance but were wholly devoted to the Tabernacle and Temple in spiritual service; the tithe also helped support widows, orphans, and aliens, who were among the most marginalized and vulnerable in ancient societies, as is still often true today (see Deuteronomy 14:27–29).

In the Old Covenant, therefore, a tithe was an offering of thanksgiving for God's many gifts, a token of giving all that we have, and even an expression of giving ourselves to the Lord. The tithe was a strict ten percent of all income from the land and the flocks. Above and beyond this, Israelites were called to offer generous care for those in special need: "For the poor will never cease out of the land; therefore I command you, You shall open wide your hand to your brother, to the needy and to the poor, in the land" (Deuteronomy 15:11; see CCC 2449).

The *Shema*, placing love for God above all things, is known as the greatest commandment (see Deuteronomy 6:4–5). But loving one's neighbor as oneself ranks second (see Leviticus 19:18, cited in Mark 12:31–33). The prophets constantly reminded God's people that prayer, sacrifice, and fasting without works of mercy were not pleasing to God. Through Hosea, God said, "I desire steadfast love and not sacrifice" (6:6). And through Isaiah, God makes clear that he was not impressed with the outward show of insincere fasting:

> Is not this the fast that I choose: to loose the bonds of wickedness, to undo the thongs of the yoke, to let the oppressed go free, and to break every yoke? Is it not to share your bread with the hungry, and bring the homeless poor into your house; when you see the naked, to cover him, and not to hide yourself from your own flesh?
>
> —Isaiah 58:6–7

Consider the following passage from Proverbs, which became instrumental in the early Church's thinking about almsgiving: "He who is kind to the poor *lends to the* LORD, and *he will repay him for his deed*" (Proverbs 19:17; emphasis added). In an act of divine condescension—God coming down to us—he willingly here seems to place himself in debt to us when we serve the poor! St. Irenaeus, writing around AD 180, explains this text as follows:

> As Solomon says, "He who is generous to the downtrodden, makes a loan to the Lord." For God, who stands in need of nothing, takes our good works to Himself for this purpose, that He may grant us a recompense of His own good things. ... As, therefore, He does not stand in need of these, yet does desire that we should render them for our own benefit, lest we be unfruitful; so did the Word give to the people that very precept as to the making of oblations, although He stood in no need of them, that they might learn to serve God: thus it is also His will that we, too, should offer a gift at the altar, frequently, and without intermission.[206]

The last line in this text, referencing our gift at the "altar," suggests that St. Irenaeus sees the fittingness of our alms as given in a *liturgical* setting—in the context of the Eucharist.[207] Living out Proverbs 19:17 is not merely a financial matter—certainly not a matter of mechanically earning one's salvation—but an act of worship, entering into the self-offering of Jesus made present in the Eucharist.

As we have discussed, the Eucharist is also our sacrifice in union with our head. In addition to placing our hearts upon the Eucharistic altar, we make a financial offering as an offering of ourselves in union with Jesus. United to Christ, our offerings become a holy sacrifice to the Father—which, as Proverbs teaches above, the Lord will pay back many times over in the age to come.

Giving as the Fruit of Faith

How necessary is a life of charity? Does what we *do* matter with respect to our own salvation?

While Jesus and St. Paul both clearly teach that salvation is a free *gift* received by faith (see Luke 8:48; Romans 3:28; Ephesians 2:8), they also teach that good works are *necessary* for salvation (see Matthew 16:27; 25:31–46; Romans 2:6, 13).

How can this be? How do faith and works fit together?

The apparent tension fades away as soon as we remind ourselves of the nature of "faith" and the transforming power of grace, especially by being attentive to the way the biblical authors are using these terms.

The Greek word for faith in the New Testament is *pistis*, which connotes far more than "belief." *Pistis* is a dynamic orientation toward God that unites us vitally to him. By faith, we, the branches, adhere to Christ, the vine, so that the vital sap of the Holy Spirit can flow into us and cause us to bear fruit. Understood in this way, faith is an all-encompassing virtue, a continual yes to the Lord by which we stand before him with an open heart. It naturally comes to fulfillment in the fruit of good works—"faith working through love" (Galatians 5:6). The only way it does not lead to good works is if the yes of faith turns into a no, and we harden our hearts to the Spirit.

To capture this dynamic, some scholars have shown that what St. Paul means by "faith" (*pistis*) is better understood in English as *allegiance*—a word that includes loyalty and fidelity.[208] In other words, "faith" for St. Paul means *faithfulness* to Jesus our King.

"Grace" means that the source of our salvation is a free gift of God. Yet grace is more than just a free gift of God's favor. It is a *"participation in the life of God"* (CCC 1997), who is working in us by the Spirit to conform us to the image of his Son. We are not passive objects in this process. Rather, as active subjects, God requires us to actively cooperate in the transforming work of his grace. We must say yes not only once but continually, always yielding to the impulse of the Spirit. For this reason, St. Paul exhorts, "Work out your own salvation with fear and trembling" (Philippians 2:12) because "God is at work in you" (2:13). Just as we must *walk* in faith, we must *work out* our salvation through love.

As some scholars have shown, the logic of "gift" in the ancient world—and especially in St. Paul—implies reciprocity. The giver also receives, and the recipient gives. Thus, the gift of the Holy Spirit empowers and enables us to do what we could not do on our own—to reciprocate the gift of grace by offering our lives back to the Lord in faithfulness and love.[209] Salvation is, on the one hand, utter gift but, at the same time, calls forth (and demands) a life of self-giving, a response made possible by the power of grace. Faith apart from works, says St. James, is "dead" (James 2:17).[210] Any branches that do not bear fruit are pruned from the vine, cast into the fire, and burned (see John 15:1–6). For St. Paul, by grace, we are "conformed to the image of his Son" (Romans 8:29).

The dynamic of the Christian life is that the gift of God's Spirit *empowers* us to live a life of faithfulness (see Ezekiel 36:27). As St. Augustine once expressed it, "The law was given that grace may be sought; and grace given that the law may be fulfilled."[211]

What About Merit?

At the end of the day, everything we are and everything we have is a free gift. Everything is ultimately based on grace. But God, as our Father, seeks to facilitate our maturation and growth in holiness and responsibility—and this is where merit comes in.

In other words, when we speak of merit, we presuppose the gratuity of this relationship that God has established. It is a little like an "allowance" that a parent might give to a child: to foster the child's maturation, a parent attaches a monetary "reward" to certain household chores. While the child "earns" the money by performing the actions, the parent does not *owe* the child money in the way that an employer owes an employee a wage.

Probably the best illustration of this is the parable of the talents in Matthew 25:14–30. The money or talents given to each of the three servants is not their own. It belongs to the master and is entrusted to their stewardship. It is not enough simply to guard the investment. Those who do are not only refused a reward; they are punished for having squandered their gift. Rather, the master expects a return on his investment and rewards those who multiply what they have been given. From those to whom much has been given, much will be expected (see Luke 12:48).

Strictly speaking, God does not *owe* us a reward—yet, in his wisdom and providence, he motivates us by showing us that certain acts are meritorious in his eyes.

What do we merit by good works? Simply, a greater share in his life and love. God's ways really do make sense!

The Need for Righteous Works

Scripture speaks of the importance and necessity of works in many places; to be sure, they must be understood within the context of our familial relationship with God. Here is a sampling of such texts—spanning the Old and New Testaments:

- To you, O Lord, belongs steadfast love. For you repay a man according to his work. (Psalm 62:12)
- And the Lord will not delay … till he repays man according to his deeds. (Sirach 35:18–19)
- Does not he who keeps watch over your soul know it, and will he not repay man according to his work? (Proverbs 24:12)
- For the Son of man is to come with his angels in the glory of his Father, and then he will repay every man for what he has done. (Matthew 16:27)
- For he will render to every man according to his works. (Romans 2:6)
- And all the churches shall know that I am he who searches mind and heart, and I will give to each of you as your works deserve. (Revelation 2:23)

None of these texts teaches that salvation can be earned in the manner of an impersonal transaction apart from Christ. Rather, as a Father, God dramatically "overpays" what our merits deserve (to say the least!). But, too often, we dilute the reality of merit and our participation in Christ's atoning work—and, thereby, undermine the importance of how we live when it comes to our salvation.

In truth, taking such passages seriously is what fueled the world-transforming power of early Christianity; taking them seriously today can dramatically facilitate our universal call to holiness and witness to the world.

Mercy: Love's Response to Suffering

Mercy is simply love's response to suffering. Confronted with suffering, love naturally seeks to relieve that suffering in any way possible. The parable of the rich man and Lazarus in Luke 16 illustrates the opposite of mercy: A wealthy man ignores the agony of a beggar at his doorstep, allowing his dogs to eat leftover food that would have relieved the beggar's hunger. The rich man is condemned for his failure to act mercifully.

So are "the goats" in the story of the last judgment told by Jesus in Matthew 25:34–46. Like the rich man, they are oblivious to the suffering of those around them. It is surprising that in Jesus' description of the Last Judgment, the goats are not condemned for sins of *commission*, for doing direct harm to others. Rather, they are condemned for sins of *omission*, for failing to do what love requires of them. A rejection of mercy can have eternal consequences because it is a rejection of Christ, who is Divine Mercy in person.

God calls us to be Christlike, and, in his providence, he teaches us that some actions—such as almsgiving—even "atone" for sin.[212] In fact, the Greek word for almsgiving (*eleemosune*) contains the root word for "mercy" (*eleos*).[213] Mysteriously, in this way, acts of mercy move the heart of God. This of course is never apart from Christ, and it needs to be understood along the lines of our discussion on merit above. This is God's fatherly way of facilitating our transformation.

In the first or early second century, the *Didache* speaks in the same vein: "If you possess anything through working with your own hands, you should give it as a ransom for your sins.[214] Equally relevant for our time is this document's prohibition against abortion and infanticide, both of which were common in Greco-Roman culture: "Do not commit an abortion, nor kill anything that has been born."[215]

The book of Tobit references the importance of prayer, fasting, and almsgiving—and expressly witnesses to the redeeming power of almsgiving:

> Prayer is good when accompanied by fasting, almsgiving, and righteousness. A little with righteousness is better than much with wrongdoing. It is better to give alms than to treasure up gold. For almsgiving delivers from death, and it will purge away every sin. Those who perform deeds of charity and of righteousness will have fulness of life.
>
> —Tobit 12:8–10

The biblical witness is clear: *What we do matters for our own salvation.* This message was embraced by the earliest Christians, who were distinguished for their charity in contrast to the pagan practices of the ancient Roman empire.[216] The early Christians were known especially for their care for the poor and sick as well as for abandoned and other unwanted infants.[217]

Exactly *how* we go about ministering to the poor depends on our circumstances and our gifts. But it is essential that we do so—that we think of our lives and money as ultimately not our own but ordered to the glory of God and the salvation of mankind. Loving our neighbor as ourselves means making their needs our own.

Christ does not propose an economic program as such; he gives us a *way*. And that way is centered on the inviolable dignity of every human life and the fact that we are, indeed, our brother's keeper (see Genesis 4:9).

The Works of Mercy

Works of mercy of various kinds are widely found in both the Old Testament and the New. Over the centuries, fourteen principal ones were enumerated—seven directed to the relief of bodily suffering and seven to spiritual suffering. They are meant to be practiced together, following Jesus' example of ministering to both body and soul.

Corporal Works of Mercy

To feed the hungry

To give drink to the thirsty

To clothe the naked

To shelter the homeless

To visit the sick

To ransom captives

To bury the dead

Six of the corporal works of mercy come from Jesus' parable of the Last Judgment in Matthew 25. The seventh, burying the dead, probably comes from the book of Tobit. The list is not exhaustive. Any work devoted to relieving physical suffering is a corporal work of mercy. Healing the sick would be included, and "ransoming captives" can mean working to save babies from abortion and young people from sex trafficking, for example.

Spiritual Works of Mercy

To instruct the ignorant

To counsel the doubtful

To admonish sinners

To bear wrongs patiently

To forgive others willingly

To comfort the afflicted

To pray for the living and the dead

Keep in mind that mercy is love's response to suffering—and not all suffering is of a physical nature. Our world is filled with lonely and anxious people, many of whom do not know that they are infinitely loved by God. Others do believe in him and want to serve him but do not know how to take that next step on the road to discipleship. They may need our counsel, our companionship, our hospitality, or our prayers.

Forgiveness and Forbearance as Works of Mercy

One of our greatest needs is to be forgiven. We may not be consciously aware that our problems have anything to do with the sins we have committed against God and others. But our baggage takes a toll. For some of us, it is a vague sense of guilt we cannot get rid of. For others, it is a callousness, a hardness of heart that comes from trying to deny or avoid thinking about our guilt. Therefore, one of the spiritual works of mercy is to forgive those who offend us. Another is to bear the faults of others patiently.

One of the ancient desert fathers explains what it means "to lay one's life down for another" (see John 15:13) in terms of forgiveness and forbearance:

> There is no greater love than that you should lay down your life for your neighbor. When you hear a complaint against you and you struggle with yourself, and do not begin to complain in return, *when you bear an injury with patience and do not look for revenge,* that is when you lay down your life for your neighbor.[218]

Another desert father defines humility in similar terms: "It is [when] you forgive a brother who has wronged you *before he is sorry.*"[219]

Forgiving those who are not sorry, bearing patiently with the faults of those who are not likely to change—these are not easy. The way of the world is to love those who love us and to resent those who have slighted us. But our Lord instructs us to the contrary:

> For if you love those who love you, what reward have you? *Do not even the tax collectors do the same?* And if you salute only your brethren, what more are you doing than others? *Do not even the Gentiles do the same?*
>
> —Matthew 5:46–47; emphasis added

Intercession as a Work of Mercy

Praying for the needs of the living and the dead is another spiritual work of mercy. Praying always (see 1 Thessalonians 5:17) means continual praise but also continual intercession. Wherever we may be—in an airport, grocery store, school, or workplace—we can be silently interceding for those around us, whether we know their specific needs or not.

When people confide in you and share a problem, tell them that you will pray for them. In fact, if circumstances allow, ask them if they would like you to pray with them right away, on the spot. You will be amazed at how many people say yes and what a moving experience it can be for both of you. Then keep the intention in your heart and pray for it while you are apart from the person. If you see the person again, ask them about the situation. You will often find that your prayer has been answered—sometimes in surprising ways.

Evangelization as a Work of Mercy

The greatest gift we can give—to the Lord or anyone else—is very often the gift of our *time* and *attention*.[220] And, if we really love people, which means we sincerely and wholeheartedly will their good, then we want them to have the greatest good—the Infinite Good, which is God himself.

Too often, when we think of evangelization, we think simply in terms of trying to get someone to join our "party," to win them to our way of "thinking," so to speak. Consequently, we lack motivation to evangelize, even finding it off-putting and distasteful, seeing it merely as an ideological imposition.

But let us think back to where we were before we really knew Jesus: Would we ever want to go back to that spot? Are we not thankful for the people in our lives who made us just a little uncomfortable—those who asked us the tough questions and prodded us to reflect a little deeper about the meaning of our lives and where we were headed?

At the end of the day, *evangelization is spiritual service*—a genuine work of mercy.

The Catholic Faith is not ours to keep for ourselves. We are stewards of something far greater than ourselves; we have received an inheritance of faith, which is meant to be passed on. In fact, it is our *duty* to pass it on. If we do not, we are ultimately failing to *love*, for we are withholding the *greatest* gift we could share with anyone—the good news that Christ has changed everything.

Our self-offering—as with Christ—serves the *whole* person, body and soul. Therefore, authentic Christian charity cannot stop with meeting the material needs of our neighbor. We must seek to share with them the pearl of great price (see Matthew 13:45–46), the gift of knowing Jesus Christ in all its fullness—which includes intimate union with him in the Eucharist.

We must pray for the boldness to share the good news with others—with love and tact, of course, but boldness nonetheless.

The Sign of the Cross and Our Share in Christ's Anointing

We were first signed with the Cross at Baptism, signifying our share in the Lord's death and resurrection. In Confirmation, we were once again marked with the Cross, this time with sacred chrism, indicating our consecration to share in the Lord's mission as priest, prophet, and king.

The works of mercy, both corporal and spiritual, are exercises of his ministry in which we share. Our intercession for the needs of all is an exercise of our priesthood. Our washing the feet of others in humble service is a sharing in Christ's kingly ministry. And our evangelization is a sharing in his prophetic mission.

Every time we make the Sign of the Cross, we invoke a summation of our entire faith and mission. God is Love, a trinitarian communion of Persons. God is not just Creator—he is Father, and he sent his Son to die our death, rise to new life, and infuse us with his very life through the gift of the Holy Spirit. Each time we make the Sign of the Cross, we are proclaiming this truth: "It is no longer I who live, but Christ who lives in me" (Galatians 2:20).

The Son is the head of the body, the Church. What happened to the head will happen to the body through the power of the Spirit—which means we will all experience both the Cross and the resurrection. Christian life is about entering the self-offering of the Son in love of God and neighbor.

God did not become man in the likes of Caesar Augustus but as a babe born in the manger. The "humility" of God shown here should be our model in all our works of mercy, including evangelization. We are not here to exert power, enjoy prestige, or win every argument. We have met Jesus Christ, and we cannot but share him with those around us; it is simply who we are as the redeemed people of God.

If we put on the humility of Christ and pray for the courage to just be ourselves, we will be amazed at the fruit the Holy Spirit will produce. But we must be patient and allow God to work in his own time. Conquest is not the goal; the only true "victory" is that won by love.

How lovely is your dwelling place, O Lord of hosts! My soul longs, yes, faints for the courts of the Lord.

— *Psalm 84:1–2*

CONCLUSION

Life Everlasting

Prayer, fasting, and almsgiving are three spiritual exercises that must be our constant companions and life-long disciplines. Why? Because life is a pilgrimage. We begin by walking, but, if St. Paul can be trusted, our faith walk must become a race (see 1 Corinthians 9:24).

To sustain us in this journey, we are given the best possible nourishment: food that is literally out of this world—the bread of heaven. Fortunately, the same God who gives us the manna from above and the stamina within is also the wind at our backs who drives us onward.

What motivates all runners is the finish line with its cheering crowds and awaiting prize. The strange thing is that we seldom think about the prize. Part of the problem is that we do not hear others talk about it much. When was the last time you had a passionate discussion with someone about heaven? And when was the last time you heard a sermon about heaven that made you want to go there?

As a teen, everlasting life did not sound all that appealing to me (Marcellino). Playing harps perched on clouds surely beat the alternative—roasting over an open fire for all eternity—but it failed to get me excited. I was looking for adventure. Yet people kept talking about heaven as "eternal rest." That only began to appeal to me about the time my wife gave birth to our fifth child.

It must be stated clearly, from the outset, that not everything having to do with God, including the world to come, can be adequately described by parallels from this world. "No eye has seen, nor ear heard, nor the heart of man conceived, what God has prepared for those who love him" (1 Corinthians 2:9). Yet we need a better impression of the prize than I had if we are to long for it so much that it serves to motivate us to run the race. The theological virtue of hope is not just the confidence that God will get us to the finish line; it means longing for it with ardent desire.

Fortunately, Scripture provides us with much more enticing images of heaven than cherubs among swirling clouds. It offers us an image from one of life's most joyous occasions—a wedding feast (see Matthew 22:1-14). The superabundance of choice wine at Cana[221] is a foreshadowing of it. Even earlier, Isaiah had explained it: "The LORD of hosts will make for all peoples a feast of fat things, a feast of choice wines—of fat things full of marrow, of choice wines well refined" (Isaiah 25:6). Every feast and celebration of this world is a pale shadow of the wedding feast of the Lamb (see Revelation 19:9). Every delight we sample in this world has diminishing returns; the first bite is always the best. And, if we eat too much, we get heartburn. Like the miraculous wine at Cana, the delights of heaven will grow ever tastier and more satisfying.

This actually gets at the authentic meaning of "eternal rest." In this world, we cannot help but be dissatisfied with any accomplishment or pleasure, for we live our lives striving for what we do not have. In this respect, we get a glimpse of the suffering inherent in being a creature who constantly yearns for more.

Nothing satisfies us for long. We look forward to graduation. Then to getting a job. But soon we long for a promotion so we can buy our first house. And then we want a bigger house. We cannot wait for vacation, perhaps visiting a new place in the world that we have always wanted to see. Yet, once we are there for a while, we cannot help but ask ourselves, "Now what?" There is a restlessness in the human heart that is a hint that we were not made for this world. As St. Augustine so aptly put it, "Our hearts are restless until they rest in you."[222]

Eternal rest means that in heaven, restlessness will be behind us. It will be time for the satisfaction of every longing—the deep peace of contentment. Paying taxes, folding laundry, and work as drudgery will be gone. Yet we will be supremely active and energized in our "rest." Our activity will be loving and enjoying God and one another. We will finally be at home, in our Father's house, safe in our Father's arms and in the arms of our brothers and sisters as well.

We crave more than anything being accepted and appreciated for who we really are—to be truly seen and understood. In this life, we can begin to experience this in our relationship with God. But seldom do we experience much of it in our human relationships, even with loved ones. So much of our baggage and the baggage of others gets in the way of our mutual love, appreciation, and communion. We misunderstand one another and annoy one another no matter how hard we try.

Now imagine all the baggage gone. All the masks removed. Every misunderstanding behind us. Imagine unimpeded intimacy with the Father, Son, and Holy Spirit and with every other member of the family. St. Paul explains it this way: "For now we see in a mirror dimly, but then face to face. Now I know in part; but then I shall understand fully, even as I have been fully understood" (1 Corinthians 13:12).

Here, by faith, we already can catch a glimpse of ourselves and other people as God sees us. There, it will not be a glimpse or a hint. It will be a panorama, brilliant in its clarity and breathtaking in its beauty. We will be amazed at the depth and goodness of each redeemed person, and each will marvel at the wonders of God and all he has done in us.

But it is not like when we see something beautiful in this life and after a while, we yawn and say, "Next!" The vision we are talking about is one of unending beauty. The vast expanse of the three divine Persons, the multitude of angels, and the countless unique, divine masterpieces—our brothers and sisters—will hold our rapt attention for all eternity. It will be an eternal *wow!* in which our amazement and excitement will not wane but ever accelerate.[223] "How lovely is your dwelling place, O LORD of hosts! My soul longs, yes, faints for the courts of the LORD" (Psalm 84:1–2).

To enter these gates of life, we need to die with Christ. We do this sacramentally in Baptism, which we then need to live out for the rest of our lives. If we preserve our baptismal garment unstained, or at least promptly wash it after soiling it, we will depart this life and cross the finish line to the cheers of the saints who await us. But if we arrive at the feast inappropriately dressed, in soiled garments, we may have to spend some time waiting in the laundry room before we are admitted to the party.[224]

And, if we reject Jesus in the least of his brothers, we may find the door barred permanently.

But it is our Father's ardent desire that we feast with him. His Son died to secure our place at the family table. And he even gives us the privilege of handing out invitations so that everyone else can come.

This is why it is worth running the race. And why we cannot keep the good news to ourselves. There is a place at the table for everyone. But how will they know unless we tell them?

Endnotes

1   See, for example, Acts 9:1–2: "Saul, still breathing threats and murder against the disciples of the Lord, went to the high priest and asked him for letters to the synagogues at Damascus, so that if he found any belonging to the Way, men or women, he might bring them bound to Jerusalem." See also Acts 19:9, 23; 22:4; 24:14, 22.

2   Paul Minear, *Images of the Church in the New Testament* (Louisville, KY: Westminster John Knox Press, 2004).

3   John Paul II, *Familiaris Consortio* (November 22, 1981), 38.

4   The Greek *apostolos* means an emissary or one who is sent out to represent another.

5   Second Vatican Council, *Dei Verbum*, Dogmatic Constitution on Divine Revelation (November 18, 1965), 10.

6   In John's Gospel (John 1:42) and in the Letters of Paul (e.g. Galatians 2:9), the Apostle Peter is called *Cephas*, the Aramaic word for "rock." Aramaic is the language Jesus probably would have spoken with his disciples, many of whom may not have known Greek.

7   Tertullian, *Apology*, 39.

8   The *Catechism of the Catholic Church* states: "The Church's first purpose is to be the sacrament of the *inner union of men with God*. Because men's communion with one another is rooted in that union with God, the Church is also the sacrament of the *unity of the human race*" (CCC 775). And elsewhere: "In her whole being and in all her members, the Church is sent to announce, bear witness, make present, and spread the mystery of the communion of the Holy Trinity" (CCC 738).

9   For more on the Church Fathers, see Marcellino D'Ambrosio, *When the Church Was Young: Voices of the Early Fathers* (Cincinnati, OH: Franciscan Media, 2014). For a complete list of the Doctors of the Church and excerpts from their writings, visit www.CrossroadsInitiative.com.

10 See CCC 76–79.

11 One easy way to see this is to realize that the canon of the Bible (the list of books making up the Old and New Testaments) is something given to us by Sacred *Tradition*.

12 CCC 78, citing *Dei Verbum* 8; italics added. See D'Ambrosio, *When the Church Was Young: Voices of the Early Fathers*, 286–294.

13 In this sense, Sacred Tradition is logically (and chronologically) prior to Sacred Scripture.

14   See Yves Congar, *Tradition and Traditions: The Biblical, Historical, and Theological Evidence for Catholic Teaching on Tradition* (New York: Simon and Schuster, 1966), 354.

15   "Christian liturgy not only recalls the events that saved us but actualizes them and makes them present. The Paschal mystery of Christ is celebrated, not repeated" (CCC 1104). And "Christ's work in the liturgy is sacramental: because his mystery of salvation is made present" (CCC 1111).

16   This is known as "the Vincentian Canon." Vincent of Lerins (AD 434), *Commonitorium*, ed. Reginald S. Moxon (Cambridge, UK: Cambridge University Press, 1915), Chapter 4.

17   Many Eastern Catholic and Orthodox Churches continue to use leavened bread in their Eucharistic liturgies.

18   ACTS Missions, Cursillo, Fellowship of Catholic University Students (FOCUS), Life Teen, National Evangelization Teams (NET), and Saint Paul's Outreach (SPO) are just a few examples of ministries with the kind of mentoring and community formation required for the passing on of the Tradition.

19   The *Catechism* basically begins with noting that human beings are essentially religious. See CCC 27–29.

20   See CCC 31–32, which notes that St. Paul (Romans 1:19–20), Augustine, and Aquinas all make this argument.

21   See Stephen C. Meyer, *Signature in the Cell: DNA and the Evidence for Intelligent Design* (New York: HarperOne, 2009).

22   C.S. Lewis, quoted by Peter Kreeft in *Fundamentals of the Faith* (San Francisco: Ignatius Press, 1988), 35. For more on the arguments for God as first cause and designer of the universe and the source of conscience, read pages 24–41 of Kreeft's book.

23   Augustine, *Confessions, 1.1.*

24   See CCC 33, 46, 1706, 1776–1802. For more on the innate moral law or conscience as evidence for the existence of God, see C.S. Lewis, *Mere Christianity* (Granite Publishers, Orem, UT 2006), I.2.

25   For more on this, see John Henry Newman's classic defense of the reasonableness of faith, *An Essay in Aid of a Grammar of Assent* (1870).

26   Thomas Aquinas, *Summa Theologiae (STh)*, I.2.3.

27   See Stephen C. Meyer, *Darwin's Doubt* (New York: HarperOne, 2010). An internet search on the author and book title will lead to short videos by the author explaining the key points of this book.

28   Robert Jastrow, *God and the Astronomers* (New York: Warner Books, 1978), 105–106. See also his book *The Enchanted Loom: Mind in the Universe* (New York: Simon & Schuster, 1981), 19.

29   For more on the attributes of the divine nature, read Frank Sheed, *Theology and Sanity* (San Francisco: Ignatius Press, 1978), 47–75.

30   While we cannot go into the Galileo case here, bear in mind that Galileo's sister was a nun, and Galileo himself remained a Catholic until his death in 1642. His tomb is inside Santa Croce Church in Florence.

31   See the Constitution on Divine Revelation of Vatican Council I, 1870, *Dei Filius,* chapter 4.

32   CCC 88–90.

33   The technical phrase used by Vatican Council I is "divine and Catholic faith" (*Dei Filius,* chapter 3) meaning the acceptance of the fullness of God's self-revelation with obedience of intellect and will, based on God's authority.

34   Stephen M. Barr, *Modern Physics and Ancient Faith* (Notre Dame, IN: University of Notre Dame Press, 2003), 9–10.

35   Ibid., 10.

36   Henri de Lubac, *The Christian Faith: An Essay on the Structure of the Apostle's Creed,* translated by Brother Richard Arnandez (San Francisco: Ignatius Press, 1986), 86.

37   For the interrogatory form of the baptismal vows, see the baptismal ceremony ca. AD 200 described in the *Apostolic Tradition of Hippolytus,* 21:6–18, excerpted in J. Neuner and J. Dupuis, eds, *The Christian Faith: Doctrinal Documents of the Catholic Church,* 7th ed (New York: Alba House, 2001), paragraph 2. Many of these elements of the ancient baptismal rite can be seen today in the Eastern Churches and the Easter vigil of the Roman rite of the Catholic Church.

38   The west is identified with Satan, the prince of darkness. See Cyril of Jerusalem, *Catechesis,* 19:2 (ca AD 350).

39   You can still see such buildings in Italy, notably the baptistry of the earliest basilica in Rome dating to the fourth century, the Basilica of St. John Lateran.

40   Cyril of Jerusalem, *Catchetical Instruction, 3, 1–3: PG 33, 426–430, ca. AD 350.*

41   *Fides informis.* See Aquinas, *STh* II–II.6.2.

42   Nicholas Ayo, *The Creed as Symbol* (Notre Dame, IN: Notre Dame University Press, 1989), 6: "The recitation of the creed by heart and in heart was a betrothal ceremony, and the *symbolum fidei* functioned as the verbal gold wedding band. Such a token is a sign of one's faith and love."

43   Augustine, *Sermo* 52.6 and 117.5, cited in CCC 230.

44   Job 36:26, cited in CCC 223.

45   Thomas Aquinas points out that our intellect never understands so much that it cannot understand more. See Aquinas, *STh* I.86.2.

46   This was never considered an absolute duty for women or for boys under age thirteen, which is still the case among Orthodox Jews.

47   Pope Francis makes this point in his encyclical *The Light of Faith*, 13.

48   See Kristen K. Deede, "The infinite qualitative difference: Sin, the self, and revelation in the thought of Søren Kierkegaard," *International Journal for Philosophy of Religion*, 53.1 (February 2003), 25–48.

49   Tertullian coined the Latin *trinitas*, and Theophilus of Antioch the Greek term *triados*.

50   One of the Old Testament "hints" is found in Genesis 1:26: "Let us make man in our own image." And, many times in the Old Testament, God's Word, Wisdom, and Spirit are spoken of as if they are in some way distinct from but equal to God.

51   See *Dives in Misericordia* (Rich in Mercy), Pope St. John Paul II's encyclical letter on God the Father (1980).

52   Elisha uses this respectful term for "my father," *abhi*, in addressing his master, Elijah. See 2 Kings 2:12.

53   See Mark 14:36; Romans 8:15; and Galatians 4:6.

54   Francis, *Lumen Fidei* (The Light of Faith), 19.

55   See the parable of the Prodigal Son in Luke 15:11–32. See also Matthew 10:30: "Even the hairs of your head are all numbered."

56   Hans Urs von Balthasar discusses the protective role of dogmas in *In the Fullness of Faith* (San Francisco: Ignatius Press, 1988), 56, 107.

57   *Dei Verbum*, 11.

58   Irenaeus commenting on Genesis, *Adversus Haereses*, 4.20.1.

59   Aquinas notes how creation is a common work of the Trinity in *STh* I.104.1.4.

60   Francis, *Laudato Si'* (May 24, 2015), 77, quoting Dante, *Paradiso*, 33.145. See Wisdom 11:24: "For you love all things that exist."

61   Many of the greatest European minds of the sixteenth and seventeenth centuries also thought this way, such as Descartes and Voltaire in France, Leibnitz and Lessing in Germany, and Locke and Hume in England.

62   John Paul II, General Audience (April 24, 1991), 6, cited by Pope Francis in *Laudato Si'*, 80. "Nature is nothing other than a certain kind of art, namely God's art" (Aquinas, *STh* I.104.1.4).

63   Though the spousal relationship is a paramount example of the fact that human nature is relational and interpersonal, even those not called to marriage nonetheless are called to live in relationship with others.

64   See Joseph Ratzinger, *Spirit of the Liturgy*, trans. John Saward (San Francisco: Ignatius Press, 2000), 26.

65   Second Vatican Council *Gaudium et Spes,* 24.

66   See *Laudato Si',* 118.

67   See *STh* I–IIae, q. 91, a. 2.

68   C.S. Lewis, *the Screwtape Letters* (New York: HarperOne, 2001). This tongue-in-cheek fictional work provides remarkable insights into temptation and the demonic realm.

69   Cf. *GS* 13 § 1.

70   Cf. Council of Trent: DS 1513; Pius XII: DS 3897; Paul VI: AAS 58 (1966) 654.

71   In the days of the Early Church, those who held this were Gnostics and Manichaeans; in the Middle Ages the proponents of this dualism were the Albigensians.

72   CCC 362–365.

73   See Ryan T. Anderson, *When Harry Became Sally* (New York: Encounter, 2018), an excellent book on the transgender issue.

74   Francis, *Laudato Si',* 6. See also 68, 69, 75, 76, and 132.

75   Francis, *Laudato Si',* 155. See also the review by Andrew Swafford of *When Harry Became Sally* at media.ascensionpress.com.

76   See John 1:1–4; 2:4; 19:26; Revelation 12:1, 5.

77   For an extensive study on the life and teaching of Jesus, see the study by Ascension Press (2020), *Jesus: The Way, the Truth, and the Life,* including the book by Marcellino D'Ambrosio by the same title.

78   God, through his prophet, had hinted to his people that they would be in for a surprise. "As the heavens are higher than the earth, so are my ways higher than your ways" (Isaiah 55:8–9).

79   For more on St. Ignatius of Antioch and the Council of Nicaea, see Marcellino D'Ambrosio, *When the Church Was Young: Voices of the Early Fathers* (Cincinnati, OH: Servant Books, 2014).

80   The New American Bible, Revised Edition translation is used here because it gets across the incomplete and fragmentary nature of the revelation prior to the coming of Jesus Christ.

81   In her prayer known as the Magnificat, Mary says "my spirit rejoices in God my Savior" (Luke 1:47). "The Holy One of Israel is your Redeemer" (Isaiah 54:5).

82   In his prayer dedicating the Jerusalem Temple in 1 Kings 8, Solomon makes it clear that the actual dwelling of the Lord is in heaven; the Temple was built as a dwelling for the Lord's Name (8:29, 48).

83   John 4:23–24. In his conversation with the Samaritan woman, Jesus says, "The hour is coming, and now is, when the true worshipers will worship the

Father in spirit and truth." In Matthew 12:6, speaking of himself, Jesus says "something greater than the temple is here." See also John 2:19–21. Speaking of his body, Jesus says, "Destroy this temple, and in three days I will raise it up."

84   The Fourth Eucharistic Prayer of the *Roman Missal*, echoing Hebrews 4:15.

85   The earliest seems to be a first-century image of Jesus in the likeness of the god Apollo, which can be viewed today in the excavations, or *scavii*, under St. Peter's Basilica. There are abundant images on the walls of the catacombs in Rome from the third century onward as well as a statue of Christ the Good Shepherd found there from the same era.

86   Ein Karem, the traditional site of Mary's visit to Elizabeth, is but a few miles from where David danced before the Ark. Elizabeth's words, "Why is this granted me, that the mother of my Lord should come to me?" (Luke 1:43), echo David's words, "How can the ark of the LORD come to me?" (2 Samuel 6:9).

87   Though foster-father is the most common way to describe Joseph's relationship to Jesus, it does not quite do justice to Joseph's role. Though he was not Jesus' biological father, he gave Jesus his name and his identity as a son of David. He was his legal, adopted Father. See Marcellino D'Ambrosio, *Jesus: The Way, the Truth, and the Life* (West Chester, PA: Ascension, 2020), chapter 3, for more.

88   The second most likely candidate for the year of the crucifixion is AD 33. For more on the ministry, life, death and resurrection of the Lord Jesus, see D'Ambrosio, *Jesus: The Way, the Truth and the Life.*

89   The earliest surviving occurrence of this phrase was in the Easter sermon of one of the early Fathers of the Church, Melito of Sardis. The phrase is used heavily by the Second Vatican Council and in the *Catechism* II.1.2, "The Paschal Mystery in the Church's Sacraments."

90   See the *Roman Missal*, Eucharistic Prayer 1: The presider, having just mentioned the saints, prays "admit us, we beseech you, into their company, not weighing our merits, but granting us your pardon."

91   See CCC 701. Note, the image of the dove appears last in the *Catechism*'s list of images for the Holy Spirit.

92   See CCC 691.

93   An analogy favored by Sheed, *Theology and Sanity*, 107. See also Romans 8:26: "We do not know how to pray as we ought, but the Spirit himself intercedes for us with sighs too deep for words."

94   See CCC 703. Each individual soul is uniquely created by God, through the Holy Spirit, at the moment of conception. This new human person is irreplaceable, with inviolable dignity.

95   Eternal life is a central theme of John's gospel and letters. See for example
      John 17:3 and 1 John 1:2.

96   See CCC 694.

97   See CCC 696.

98   See for example Acts 4:13, which speaks of the "boldness of Peter and John,"
      and 4:29, "to speak your word with all boldness." See also Acts 14:3.

99   See CCC 692. See also John 14:16; 16:7.

100   See C.S. Lewis, *The Great Divorce: A Dream* (San Francisco: HarperCollins,
      2001), 75: "There are only two kinds of people in the end: those who say to
      God, 'Thy will be done,' and those to whom God says, in the end, 'Thy will be
      done.' All that are in Hell, choose it. Without that self-choice there could be no
      Hell. No soul that seriously and constantly desires joy will ever miss it. Those
      who seek find. Those who knock it is opened."

101   CCC 1082.

102   They are called "theological" virtues because they are supernatural gifts
      from God that lead us to God. The four cardinal virtues of justice, prudence,
      temperance, and fortitude are natural virtues that even unbelievers can
      recognize to be of the essence of human greatness. The Spirit helps us develop
      these as well. For more on the virtues, see Peter Kreeft, *Back to Virtue* (San
      Francisco: Ignatius Press, 1992).

103   On the seven gifts, see Aquinas, *STh* II–II.8, 9, 19, 45, 52, 121, 139.

104   CCC 768 calls this a hierarchical gift and distinguishes it from the charismatic
      gifts, which it associates with gifts freely poured out directly by the spirit on
      the baptized. But, in the New Testament, the ordination of Timothy is also
      described in terms of a gift or charism (*charisma*) in 2 Timothy 1:6.

105   See CCC 799–801.

106   This limitation is shared by most modern European languages—where
      Latin and Greek have endings on nouns to show what role they play in a
      given sentence (declensions), modern languages do not and so have to use
      prepositions like "in" more frequently, as in "I believe in the Church."

107   CCC 750: "In the Apostles' Creed we profess 'one Holy Church' (*Credo . . .
      Ecclesiam*), and not to believe *in* the Church, so as not to confuse God with his
      works and to attribute clearly to God's goodness *all* the gifts he has bestowed
      on his Church" (*Roman Catechism* I, 10, 22). For more on this see Lubac, *The
      Christian Faith,* 203–216.

108   See CCC 796.

109   Francis, *Light of Faith,* 47.

110   Cyprian, *On the Unity of the Church,* 6.

111 In both cases the RSV translates the word *mysteria* as "secrets," which gets across an aspect of this term "mystery" but not its full range of meanings.

112 See 1 Corinthians 2:1, 7 and 4:1. In the first two instances, the RSV translates the word mystery as "the testimony" and "a secret and hidden wisdom." In 4:1, it does finally use the word in "mysteries of God."

113 Luke 5:17: "And the power of the Lord was with him to heal."

114 The adjective "ecclesial" comes from the Greek word for church, *ekklesia*.

115 The New Testament Greek word for this is *koinonia*, which can also be translated "fellowship."

116 See CCC 817–822.

117 Irenaeus, *Against Heresies, Lib. 4, 20, 5–7.*

118 See CCC 823–828.

119 The Latin word *persona* and the equivalent Greek term *prosopon* originally referred to characters on a stage. It was Tertullian who first used the word in its modern sense to distinguish the three Persons of the Holy Trinity. See Metropolitan John Zizioulas, *Being As Communion: Studies in Personhood and the Church* (Crestwood, NY: St. Vladimir's Seminary Press, 1997), 27–49.

120 Just as he did that day at Caesarea Philippi (see Matthew 16:16).

121 See CCC 830–848.

122 CCC 857–865.

123 See Thérèse of Lisieux, *The Story of a Soul.*

124 See CCC 1069, citing *Sacrosanctum Concilium,* 7.

125 See John 15, cited in CCC 1108.

126 See CCC 1324; *Sacrosanctum Concilium,* 10.

127 Indeed, "mystagogy" (i.e., study of the "mysteries") is the term coined in the early Church to explain the theology of the sacraments by recourse to the typology of the Bible (e.g., the Flood in Noah's day and Baptism; see 1 Peter 3:20–21). See CCC 1075.

128 See Scott W. Hahn, *Kinship by Covenant: A Canonical Approach to the Fulfillment of God's Saving Promises* (New Haven, CT: Yale University Press, 2009) and Scott Hahn, *A Father Who Keeps His Promises: God's Covenant Love in Scripture* (Cincinnati, OH: Servant Books, 1998).

129 See Scott Hahn, *Swear to God: The Promise and the Power of the Sacraments* (New York: Doubleday, 2004).

130 Rites, ceremonies, and blessings instituted by the Church rather than Christ are nonetheless wonderful. Those instituted by Christ are called sacraments, while those instituted by the Church are called sacramentals.

131   Cited in Jean Daniélou, *The Bible and the Liturgy* (Notre Dame, IN: Notre Dame Press, 1956), 44.

132   See CCC 1010.

133   The *Catechism* explains, "Confirmation perfects Baptismal grace; it is the sacrament which gives the Holy Spirit in order to root us more deeply in the divine filiation" (CCC 1316).

134   "Christ" means "anointed one" and is the Greek equivalent of the Hebrew "messiah." Hence, as the following quote from St. Cyril describes, this sacramental "anointing" makes us little "Christs" in Jesus Christ. It is also worth noting that Acts 8:14–16 recounts Christians receiving the gift of the Spirit after Baptism, suggestive of the reality of Confirmation.

      While preparing candidates for Baptism and Confirmation in the fourth century, St. Cyril of Jerusalem wrote:

> You were made Christs when you received the sacrament of the Holy Spirit [i.e., Confirmation]. ... And He [Jesus], having bathed in the Jordan, the Holy Spirit descended personally upon Him, Like resting on Like. And you also, when you came out of the pool of the sacred water, you received the anointing, the sacrament of that which Christ was anointed, I mean to say, the Holy Spirit. (Daniélou, *The Bible and the Liturgy*, 118)

      Cyril continues:

> As it has been granted to you in Baptism to be crucified with Him, buried with Him, risen again with Him in a certain imitation, so it is with the chrism [i.e., Confirmation]. He was anointed with the spiritual oil of exultation, that is to say, with the Holy Spirit, called the Oil of Exultation because He is the source of spiritual joy; and you, you have been anointed with perfumed oil, and become participants in Christ. (Daniélou, *The Bible and the Liturgy*, 118)

      Daniélou comments:

> This passage is one of the most remarkable in sacramental theology. First of all, it states clearly what a sacrament is: a real participation in the grace of Christ, by a sacramental imitation of His life. ... As Baptism configures us to Christ dead and risen again, so Confirmation configures us to Christ anointed by the Holy Spirit. The Baptism of Christ, followed by the descent of the Holy Spirit, is thus seen to be a prefiguration of His death followed by His royal enthronement, of which the Christian in turn partakes by means of the two sacraments of water and of the anointing." (Daniélou, *The Bible and the Liturgy*, 118)

135 "Ordinary minister" means the normal, proper, and preferred one. When a bishop cannot be present, a priest may confirm validly, but only using chrism consecrated by the bishop.

136 When anyone over the age of reason is baptized, Baptism is immediately followed by Confirmation and First Communion. In some jurisdictions, this order has been restored, so that Confirmation precedes First Communion for young people who were baptized as infants.

137 The passage in Mark 6:13 is not the sacrament of Anointing of the Sick, since Jesus has not yet died and risen (and sent the Spirit). This anointing was a prefiguration of the sacrament, not the sacrament itself.

138 Jacques Philippe, *Searching for and Maintaining Peace: A Small Treatise on Peace of Heart* (Staten Island, NY: St. Paul, 2002), 49.

139 See CCC 1521, 1523, 1525.

140 Francis, *The Twelve Pillars* (January 22, 2016), https://www.vatican. va/content/francesco/en/cotidie/2016/documents/papa-francesco-cotidie_20160122_the-twelve-pillars.html.

141 John the Baptist describes Jesus as the bridegroom (see John 3:29–30), and Jesus confirms this theme in the parables of the wedding feast (see Matthew 22:1–14) and the wise and foolish virgins (see Matthew 25:1–13). The image also appears in his answers to those who want to know why John's followers fast and his do not (see [Matthew 9:15; Mark 2:19–20]). Some of the Church Fathers understand the opening lines of Song of Songs ("O that you would kiss me with the kisses of your mouth" [Song of Songs 1:2]) as finding fulfillment in the Holy Eucharist (see Daniélou, *The Bible and the Liturgy*, 204–205).

142 See Craig A. Evans and N.T. Wright, *Jesus, the Final Days: What Really Happened*, ed. Troy A. Miller (Louisville, KY: Westminster John Knox, 2009), 89–90.

143 Daniélou, *The Bible and the Liturgy*, 17; emphasis added.

144 See Andrew Swafford and Jeff Cavins: *Hebrews: The New and Eternal Covenant* (West Chester, PA: Ascension, 2020), 57–60.

145 Irenaeus, *Against Heresies*, 4, 18, 5, cited in CCC 1327.

146 Mishnah 10:5, cited from *The Mishnah: A New Translation*, trans. Jacob Neusner (New Haven, CT: Yale University Press, 1988), 250. The Mishnah is a compilation of ancient Jewish oral tradition dating to centuries before Christ, finally written down around AD 200.

147 The English word "Easter" obviously does not retain this connection, making it harder for English speakers to be aware of this Passover background to the central mystery of our salvation.

148   See Daniélou, *The Bible and the Liturgy*, 262–286.

149   See CCC 1360. Eucharist means first of all "thanksgiving."

150   See *Sacrosanctum Concilium*, 7.

151   Offering an outward sign of peace is supposed to reflect an inward decision
       that we forgive all those who have offended us, accepting forgiveness of those
       we have offended, and are, therefore, free to approach the altar.

152   Christ is the only priest, as St. Thomas Aquinas points out: "Only Christ is the
       true priest, the others being only his ministers" (CCC 1545).

153   *Dei Verbum*, 21.

154   For a superb and extensive examination of Scripture in the prayers of the
       Mass of the Roman rite, see Edward Sri, *A Biblical Walk through the Mass*, rev.
       ed. (West Chester, PA: Ascension Press, 2021).

155   Thomas Aquinas, *STh* III, 65,1, cited in CCC 1210.

156   Meaning transformation of substance. See CCC 1376, 1413.

157   In a number of well-known Eucharistic miracles, such as those of Bolsena or
       Lanziano, a physical transformation has apparently taken place.

158   See CCC 1391–1401.

159   See CCC 1127–1128. The technical way to put this that the sacraments are
       efficacious *ex opere operato*.

160   See CCC 1128, 1395, 1415.

161   See Philip J. Long, *Jesus the Bridegroom: The Origin of the Eschatological Feast as
       a Wedding Banquet in the Synoptic Gospels* (Eugene, OR: Pickwick, 2013), 52:
       "Exod 24:1-11 is perhaps *the most important text* for understanding the idea of
       an eschatological banquet" (emphasis added).

162   The word for "reproach" here (*herpah*) generally refers to "sin" and "shame."

163   Other Jewish texts outside the Bible join these motifs, such as the messianic
       banquet and hope for resurrection. Here is a passage from a text known as
       1 Enoch, which witnesses to Jewish thought around the time of Christ: "The
       righteous and elect ones shall be *saved on that day ... they shall eat and rest
       and rise with that Son of Man* forever and ever. The *righteous and elect ones shall
       rise from the earth* and shall cease being of downcast face. They shall wear
       the garments of glory. These garments of yours shall become the *garments of
       life* from the Lord of the Spirits. Neither shall your garments wear out, nor
       your glory come to an end before the Lord of the Spirits" (*1 Enoch.* 62:13–16;
       emphasis added). The importance of a text like this is that such Jewish hopes
       were alive and well at the time of Jesus. Jesus here *taps into*—and *transcends*—
       these Jewish expectations of his day.

164   See also 1 Corinthians 9:24–27 and 2 Timothy 4:7.

165   Joseph Ratzinger, *Introduction to Christianity*, trans. J.R. Foster (San Francisco: Ignatius Press, 1990), 43.

166   For more on the moral life, see Andrew Swafford, *John Paul II to Aristotle and Back Again: A Christian Philosophy of Life* (Eugene, OR: Wipf and Stock, 2015) and Edward Sri, *The Art of Living: The Cardinal Virtues and the Freedom to Love* (San Francisco: Ignatius Press, 2021).

167   A practical way to help apply God's truth and the authentic movement of the Holy Spirit is to ask someone to serve as a spiritual director. Spiritual direction is a form of friendship with Christ whereby a person freely asks someone more mature in the spiritual life for regular guidance. If the director is a priest, the sacrament of Penance may be integrated within a spiritual direction session. But this is not at all a requirement. Receiving spiritual direction from a deacon, a wise religious sister or brother, or an experienced layperson is a time-honored practice.

168   Augustine, *Confessions*, 8.7.

169   CCC 521, citing St. John Eudes, *LH*, Week 33, Friday, OR.

170   By "world" here John means the tyranny of sin and the Evil One, not God's good creation.

171   This is made clear by several biblical texts such as Sirach 14:8–10 as well as Proverbs 22:9 and 27:20.

172   CCC 398, citing St. Maximus the Confessor, *Ambigua*: PG 91, 1156C; cf. *Gen* 3:5. The *Catechism* explains, "In that [original] sin man *preferred* himself to God and by that very act scorned him. He chose himself over and against God, against the requirements of his creaturely status and therefore against his own good. Constituted in a state of holiness, man was destined to be fully 'divinized' by God in glory. Seduced by the devil, he wanted to 'be like God,' but 'without God, before God, and not in accordance with God.'"

173   The general pattern can be observed in all Catholic rites, both East and West, though specific prayers like the *Gloria* vary from rite to rite.

174   The Penitential Rite in the Eucharist does remit venial sin. We must confess mortal sin in the sacrament of Penance and do so before we present ourselves for Communion. It is also highly recommended that we confess venial sins in confession and do so regularly.

175   Even in the Roman rite of private confession, the priest is given several optional Scripture texts to begin with. Due to the number of penitents and lack of time, priests rarely make use of them.

176   James 1:19: "Be quick to hear, slow to speak." This is good advice with regard to our relationships with God as well as with other people.

177 The text of the *Didache*, which probably reflects Christian practice in the late
    first and early second centuries, suggests that the Our Father replaced the
    recitation of the *Shema* early on.

178 In the Revised Standard Version of the Bible, second Catholic edition, the
    "Song of the Three Young Men" can be found in the italicized verses of Daniel
    3. In the New American Bible, it appears at Daniel 3:52–90.

179 Free apps include Laudate and iBreviary; Universalis requires a small fee.
    "Sing the Hours," a chanted version of Lauds and Vespers in English with
    a little Latin, is available daily online and as an app, and Fr. Kevin Vogel's
    chanted Compline for each night of the week is available on YouTube.

180 Originally, this was an informal process, led by the Spirit. It is often described
    as occurring in four successive phases: *lectio* (reading), *metitatio* (meditation),
    oratio (prayer) and *contemplatio* (contemplation). This should not be thought
    of, however, as a formal, systematic schema that always must be carried out in
    rigid fashion. *Lectio divina* is essentially dwelling on a text prayerfully, letting
    God's word penetrate you and transform you.

181 For a meditation before each decade, see Matt Fradd, *Pocket Guide to the
    Rosary* (West Chester, PA: Ascension: 2019). For a Rosary with a Scripture
    between each Hail Mary, see *The Scriptural Rosary* (Glenview, IL: Christianica
    Center, 2005). Finally see Edward Sri, *Praying the Rosary Like Never Before*
    (Cincinnati, OH: Franciscan Media, 2018).

182 For a wonderful introduction to the Jesus prayer as the prayer of the heart,
    see the anonymous work titled *The Way of the Pilgrim,* trans. Helen Bacovcin
    (New York: Doubleday Image, 1978).

183 CCC 2777.

184 See Matthias Scheeben, *The Mysteries of Christianity*, trans. Cyril Vollert (St.
    Louis, MO: Herder, 1946), 486–487.

185 "Every baptized person is called to be a 'blessing,' and to bless" (CCC 1669).

186 Blessings for use by lay people can be found in the *Shorter Book of Blessings*
    (Totowa, NJ: Catholic Book Publishing, 2020) and *Catholic Household Blessings
    and Prayers* (Washington, DC: USCCB, 2020).

187 See, for example, 1 Samuel 31:13; 2 Samuel 1:12; and 2 Samuel 3:35.

188 See Judges 20:26; 1 Samuel 7:6; 2 Chronicles 20:3; Judith 4:9; Esther 4:16;
    Jeremiah 14:12; 36:6; Joel 1:14; 2:12, 15; Jonah 3:5; 1 Maccabees 3:47; 2
    Maccabees 13:12.

189 The inspiration for Paul and Barnabas's first great missionary journey came
    to the church at Antioch while they were praying and fasting. After further
    prayer and fasting, the church sent them off. See Acts 13:1–3.

190 Both quoting Deuteronomy 8:3.

191   St. Thomas Aquinas points to this passage in terms of our mourning and seeing the sorrowful truth when we sin by making creatures, instead of God, our last and final end (see *STh* II–II.9.4).

192   Pope Benedict XVI, *Jesus of Nazareth*, vol. 1, *From the Baptism in the Jordan to the Transfiguration* (New York: Doubleday, 2007), 86; emphasis added.

193   Jonathan T. Pennington, *The Sermon on the Mount and Human Flourishing: A Theological Commentary* (Grand Rapids, MN: Baker Academic, 2017), 71. This "wholeness" is "Godward virtue" (205). See also Amy-Jill Levine, *Sermon on the Mount: A Beginner's Guide to the Kingdom of Heaven* (Nashville, TN: Abingdon, 2020), 52–53.

194   See John Paul II, *Veritatis Splendor*, 7.

195   C.S. Lewis, *Mere Christianity* (San Francisco: HarperCollins, 2001), 78.

196   C.S. Lewis, *Screwtape Letters* (San Francisco: HarperCollins, 2001), 162. See also Andrew Swafford, *Spiritual Survival in the Modern World: Insights from C.S. Lewis' Screwtape Letters* (Eugene, OR: Wipf and Stock, 2016), 111–115.

197   Josef Pieper, *Four Cardinal Virtues*, trans. Richard Winston (South Bend, IN: University of Notre Dame Press, 1966), 181.

198   See Swafford, *Spiritual Survival in the Modern World*, 69–73.

199   Lewis, *Mere Christianity*, 79.

200   Council of Trent, Decree on the Sacrament of Penance, ch. IX.

201   Walter J. Ciszek, *With God in Russia* (1964; repr., New York: HarperOne, 2017), 14.

202   Ibid., 19. This was in 1938.

203   Ibid., 31.

204   Ibid., 134, original emphasis.

205   Ibid., 165. "For what can ultimately trouble the soul that accepts every moment of every day as a gift from the hands of God and strives always to do his will? ... Nothing, not even death, can separate us from God" (Ciszek, 208).

206   Irenaeus, *Against Heresies* 4.18; emphasis added.

207   See Gary A. Anderson, *Sin: A History* (New Haven, CT: Yale University Press, 2009), 166: "In giving alms to the poor we are making a loan to the Son of Man. But it is important to note that Irenaeus thinks of this 'loan' not as a financial matter but as *liturgical* act" (emphasis added).

208   Matthew Bates, *Salvation by Allegiance Alone: Rethinking Faith, Works, and the Gospel of Jesus the King* (Grand Rapids, MI: Baker, 2017).

209   See John Barclay, *Paul and the Gift* (Grand Rapids, MI: Eerdmans, 2015), 492.

210   St. Paul gets at the same reality when he bookends his famous letter to the Romans with the phrase the "obedience of faith" (Romans 1:5; 16:26).

211   Augustine, *On the Spirit and the Letter* 19.34.

212   See Sirach 3:30 and Tobit 4:10–11. James 2:25 indicates that Rahab's
       hospitality was redemptive and even atoned for sin. See also Hebrews 11:31.
       Daniel 4:24–27 is another example, with Daniel instructing Nebuchadnezzar
       to atone for sin through almsgiving; this comes out especially in the
       Septuagint: "Redeem your sins [*lutrosai*] by almsgiving [*eleemosune*]" (Daniel
       4:27, author's translation).

213   We say the verbal form of this word at Mass when we sing *Kyrie, eleeson*,
       which is taken directly from Scripture (see, for example, Matthew 20:31;
       Luke 17:13). Normally, we spell "Lord, have mercy" with an *i* (*eleison*) for
       pronunciation purposes; here, we spell it "ee" to accurately represent the
       Greek, which makes the connection clearer between "almsgiving" (*eleemosune*)
       and "mercy" (*eleeos*)—or "have mercy" (*eleeson*).

214   *Didache* 4.6, cited in *Clement of Rome and the Didache: A New Translation
       and Theological Commentary*, trans. Kenneth J. Howell (Zanesville, OH:
       ChResources, 2012), 141. Similarly, St. Gregory the Great writes, "Those who
       give mercifully should be advised that *as they redeem the sins of their past
       through almsgiving*, they not commit further sins that will require redemption"
       (Gregory, *The Book of Pastoral Rule*, 143).

215   *Didache* 2.2, cited in Howell, 139–140.

216   See Giambrone, *Sacramental Charity, Creditor Christology, and the Economy
       of Salvation in Luke's Gospel*, 175–182. Gary A. Anderson, *Sin: A History*,
       154–160. From a sociological perspective, see also Rodney Stark, *The Rise of
       Christianity: How the Obscure, Marginal Jesus Movement Became the Dominant
       Religious Force in the Western World in a Few Centuries* (San Francisco: Harper,
       1997), 73–94. Jews, drawing from the same Old Testament tradition, were also
       notable for their charity in the ancient world.

217   Stark, *Rise of Christianity*, 73–94.

218   Benedicta Ward, ed. *The Desert Fathers: Sayings of the Early Christian Monks*
       (New York: Penguin Press, 2003), 178–179; emphasis added. The desert father
       quoted here is anonymous.

219   Ibid., 163; emphasis added.

220   Jacques Philippe, *Thirsting for Prayer* (New Rochelle, NY: Scepter, 2014), 12.

221   The six jars held twenty to thirty gallons each. An example of such a massive
       stone jar from around the time of Christ is on display in the Church of the
       First Miracle in Cana, Israel.

222   Augustine, *Confessions* 1.1.1.

223   For fiction that can help stimulate your imagination along these lines, see C.S. Lewis, *The Great Divorce*, as well as the final chapters of *The Last Battle*, the last book of his Chronicles of Narnia.

224   See Matthew 22:11–14. In its teaching on Purgatory, the Church is quite modest. Despite many popular stories and reputed visions, the Church teaches that purification after death is needed by some souls and that we should pray for them. Though purifying fire is a biblical image used to describe this process, the Church does not describe the exact nature of the process. As for the living, the Church offers every aid in sacraments, spiritual exercises, and indulgences, so that we have every opportunity to take care of purification here and, thus, to avoid any delay in entering into glory. See CCC 1030–1032.

Meet the Authors

Dr. Marcellino D'Ambrosio ("Dr. Italy") received his Ph.D. in historical theology from The Catholic University of America under the direction of Avery Cardinal Dulles and has had a prolific career as a Catholic author, internationally-respected speaker, pilgrimage leader, and university professor. He is the co-founder and director of *The Crossroads Initiative*, the author of five books and hundreds of articles, and a regular guest on both secular and Catholic TV and radio programs. In 2004, Dr. D'Ambrosio co-authored the *New York Times* bestseller *A Guide to the Passion: 100 Questions about The Passion of the Christ* with Ascension Founder Matt Pinto. In 2019, Dr. D'Ambrosio published the groundbreaking Bible study on the life of Jesus Christ filmed in the Holy Land, *Jesus: The Way, the Truth, and the Life*, presenting alongside Jeff Cavins and Dr. Edward Sri.

Dr. D'Ambrosio is currently a professor of theology at the Catholic Distance University. He and his wife Susan reside in Dallas, Texas.

Dr. Andrew Swafford is a professor of theology at Benedictine College. He is a general editor and contributor to *The Great Adventure Catholic Bible* as well as author and host of several Ascension Bible studies, including *Hebrews: The New and Eternal Covenant* and *Romans: The Gospel of Salvation*. In addition to his work with Ascension, Dr. Swafford has written several books on nature and grace, Pope St. John Paul II, and modern spirituality. He holds a doctorate in sacred theology from the University of St. Mary of the Lake and a master's degree in Old Testament and Semitic languages from Trinity Evangelical Divinity School. He is a member of the Society of Biblical Literature and the Academy of Catholic Theology, and a senior fellow at the St. Paul Center for Biblical Theology. He is a practitioner of Brazilian Jiu Jitsu and lives with his wife Sarah and their five children in Atchison, Kansas.